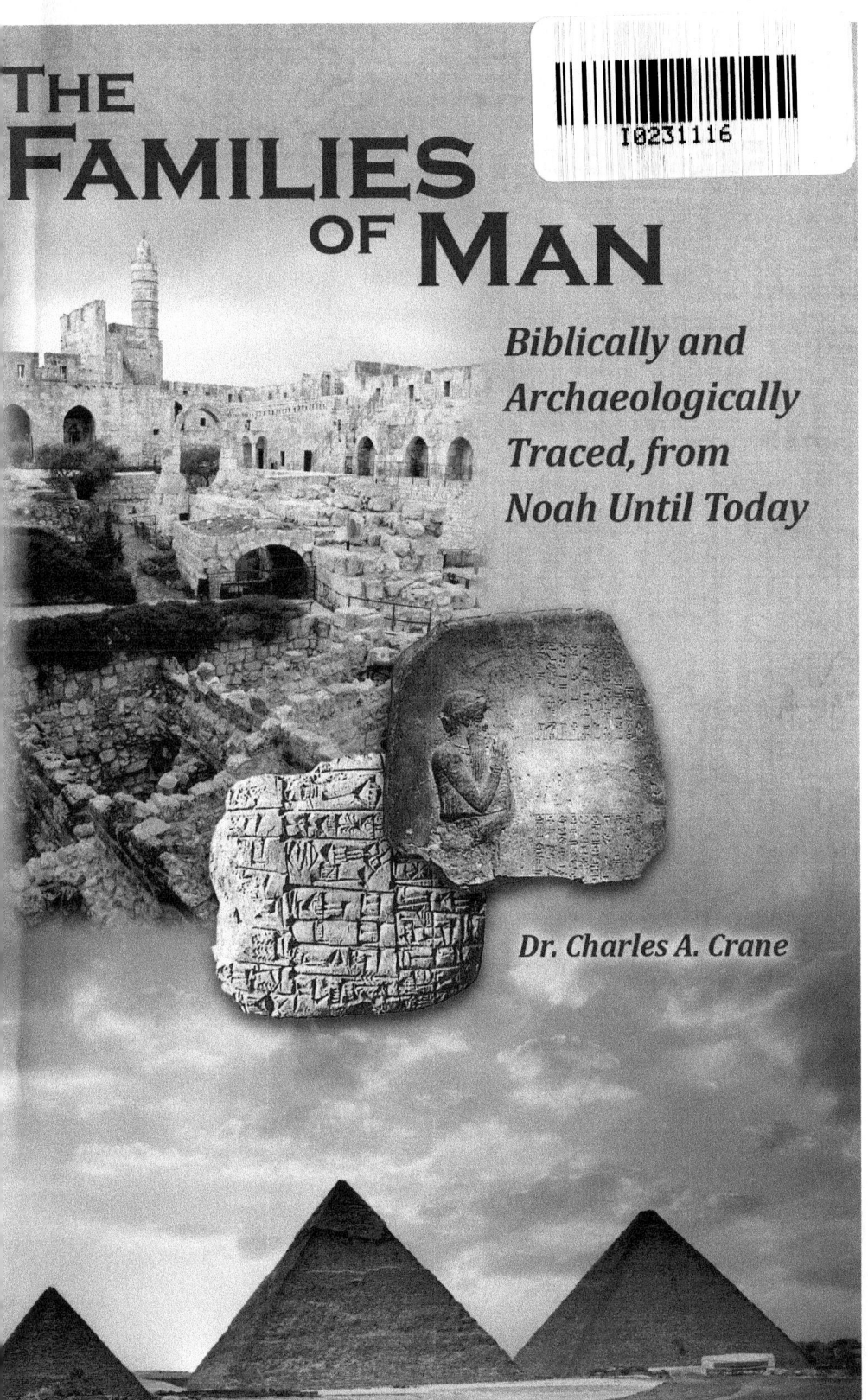

THE FAMILIES OF MAN

Biblically and Archaeologically Traced, from Noah Until Today

Dr. Charles A. Crane

BIBLE PROOF SERIES

BIBLICAL ARCHAEOLOGY

OR

THE FAMILIES OF MAN BIBLICALLY AND
ARCHAEOLOGICALLY TRACED

Dr. Charles A. Crane, D. Min.

2017

Biblical Archaeology or The Families of Man Biblically Traced is available at special quantity discounts for bulk purchase for sales promotions, premiums, fund-raising, and educational needs. For details write Endurance Press, 577 N Cardigan Ave Star, ID 83669.

Visit Endurance Press' website at www.endurancepress.com

Biblical Archaeology or
The Families of Man Biblically
and Archaeologically Traced

PUBLISHED BY ENDURANCE PRESS
577 N Cardigan Ave
Star, ID 83669 U.S.A.

All views expressed within are the view of the author and do not necessarily reflect the views of the publisher.

© Dr. Charles A. Crane 2017

All rights reserved. Except for brief excerpts for review purposes, no part of this book may be reproduced or used in any form without prior written permission from the publisher.
ISBN 978-09988756-2-0

"Scripture quotations taken from the English Standard Version,

Copyright 2001, by Crossway Publishing,

a ministry of Good News Publishers.

Quoted by permission."

®2017 Dr. Charles A Crane
Printed in the United States of America
First Edition 2017

TABLE OF CONTENTS

Preface 11

Chapter One—Introduction to Archaeology 13

    What is the purpose of studying biblical archaeology?
    Biblical archaeology
    People who began this work
    The primary lands of the Bible
    Dating of archaeological sites
    Carbon 14 dating
    Summary

Chapter Two—The Flood of Noah 25
    Evidence for a worldwide flood
    The formation of petroleum deposits
    Population on the earth in Noah's day

Chapter Three—Noah's Ark 38
    The 5000 year old mystery
    Evidence for the ark's existence

Chapter Four—The Tower of Babel 46
    Two important things
    The Tower of Babel
    Where were the people scattered?

Chapter Five—Ebla in Syria 54
    Archaeological findings of great value
    Ebla's location
    Massive library found
    The language of Ebla
    Dates of this civilization and the area it ruled
    Related to the Hittite Kingdom of Turkey

The value of the tablets
　　Ebla, Egypt, and China's beginnings
　　Evolutionists' theories proven untrue

Chapter Six—Ur of the Chaldees. 63
　　Finding the Ur of Abraham and Sarah
　　Archaeological excavation
　　Hammurabi's Code
　　Libraries were common
　　Abraham distressed by Ur's sinfulness
　　The ruins of Ur
　　Time line chart from the Flood to Pyramids of Giza

Chapter Seven—Early Canaanite Cities or Tels. 72
　　The founding of a tel
　　Tels natural tendency to grow
　　The death of tels
　　The value of tels today
　　Let's examine three well-known tels

Chapter Eight—Sodom, Gomorrah, and Petra. 78
　　Where did Moab, Ammon, and Edom come from?
　　Looking for Sodom and Gomorrah
　　How were they destroyed?
　　Petra and the descendants of Lot and Esau
　　Sier, Petra, and Sela
　　Concluding thoughts

Chapter Nine—Egypt, the Pyramids, and Goshen. 86
　　Egyptian Pyramids
　　Pyramids and Pharaohs
　　The Step Pyramid
　　The Bent Pyramid
　　The Red Pyramid
　　The Land of Goshen

Chapter Ten—Jericho. 96
　　The Red Sea crossing

Uncertain where Israel crossed
Jericho
History and age of Jericho
Archaeological excavations
God placed a curse on the rebuilder

Chapter Eleven—Ai and Gibeon........................104
Ai
Gibeon
The sun stood still and huge hail
Finding Gibeon

Chapter Twelve—Megiddo and Hazor.................112
Megiddo, the meaning of the name
History of Megiddo
The water system
James Michener and his book *The Source*
Tel Megiddo
The true and untrue

Chapter Thirteen—Writing, Inscriptions and Languages...120
Could Adam and Eve read and write?
The Behistun Rock
The Rosetta Stone
The Amarna Tablets and the Habiru
Examples of ancient writing
The Anvil of God's Word

Chapter Fourteen—Jerusalem........................142
The ancient history of Jerusalem
The Gihon Spring
King David and the Gihon
The Warren Shaft and the Gihon
King Solomon at the Gihon
King Hezekiah and the Gihon
The Garden of Gethsemane
The Courtyard of the Praetorium Guard
The High Priest's house and dungeon

    Calvary and the Garden Tomb
    Abraham and Melchizedek
    The Cross Was His Own

Chapter Fifteen—Nineveh and Babylon. 156
    Nineveh
    Nineveh's origin and history
    Babylon
    Geography and history of Babylon
    Nebuchadnezzar captures Judah with Daniel
    Babylon's earlier history
    Archaeology of Babylon

Chapter Sixteen—Bible Origins and the Dead Sea Scrolls. . 168
    The Bible books and writers
    The Great Synagogue
    The preservation of the Old Testament text
    Qumron
    Finding the Dead Sea Scrolls
    The value of the scrolls

Chapter Seventeen—Herod the Great—The Builder. . . . 179
    The Olivet Discourse
    Herod the Great
    Herod the Great's building projects
    The Herodium
    Masada
    Machaerus
    Gamla
    Conclusions to be drawn

Chapter Eighteen—Where We've Been and Need to Go. . . 193
    A review of where we have been so far
    There is much work left to be done
    Conclusions
    The Bible Stands

Bibliography. 205

Preface

This book has had its origin from a series of Bible School lessons that have been called The Bible Proof Series. The first series became a book titled *The Bible, the True and Reliable Word of God*. The second series was titled *Prophetic Proof that Jesus Is the Messiah*. This third series has shown that archaeology has substantiated the Bible from Genesis through Revelation.

It is the author's contention that there is no significant archaeological evidence of civilization before the Flood of Noah, since the world was thoroughly destroyed. Yes, remains of various kinds of animals have been found, but not cities, graveyards, or evidence of organized civilization.

Therefore this book begins with Noah and his three sons' families. There is significant evidence to substantiate the biblical history, not only for the Flood, but for things like the Tower of Babel, early cities, very early writing, and much more.

An interesting sidelight to this study is to see how humans spread over the earth after the Flood. Searching the oldest histories and most ancient archaeological sites has provided significant insights into the origins of the world's oldest civilizations. This information is summarized in this book.

The author struggled with whether to include the many pictures which were shown in the classes. The question was whether to include them at significant cost increase to the book, not only in dollars, but in the size of the book. Realizing the futility of trying to show hundreds of pictures, it was decided that most people now have computers and can easily find a wealth of pictures of the archaeological sites studied. It is suggested that the reader take the chapter heading and do an internet search for it and when the site comes up look at the heading that says pictures. There you will find a wealth of

BIBLICAL ARCHAEOLOGY

information and pictures and at no additional cost. This effort should be well worth your investment of time.

The author appreciates the help of many people in producing this book. Janet Colburn, an executive assistant, has spent many hours reading and correcting the manuscript, and designed the cover. Others have also helped: Barbie Getchell, archaeologist; Dr. Ed Stevens, long-time college professor; Dr. Neal Rusco, professor of language at the College of Idaho; and of course Margaret Crane, the author's wife, who has read and corrected the text.

The author does not claim that some of the information contained is not still open to discussion, many of the subjects are. It is his belief that this book, though, furthers the study and hopefully will encourage much more research, especially in regard to the lineage of some of the more obscure families of mankind, like the primitive people of Alaska, North and Central America, the Aztecs, Incas, and Peruvians. With modern tools, such as DNA, it should be possible to link even tribes like the Polynesians and ancient Aborigines of Australia back to their biblical roots.

It is hoped that this book adds valuable information that further illustrates how historically accurate the Bible is. As Jesus said, "The Scriptures cannot be broken" (John 10:35).

Dr. Charles A. Crane

Chapter One

Introduction to Archaeology

On the evening news, it was reported that American Christians who attend church regularly are woefully uninformed about the Bible. This has been confirmed by the author's sixty years of teaching in the church. The result of this lack of biblical knowledge is that their Christian faith is weak ("Faith comes by hearing and hearing by the word of Christ." Romans 10:17)[1] and they do not have the joy or productivity they should have in their Christian lives. Their lack of knowledge leaves them vulnerable to many errors.

In this book the goal will be to look at a few of the many archaeological proofs of the historical accuracy of the Bible and to trace the families of mankind as they spread across the earth. We will begin with an introduction to the study of biblical archaeology and give a few examples of what this study has shown about our Bible. The prayer is that this will augment the foundation of your faith and produce fruit in your life. Archaeology has produced many astounding discoveries.

Abraham Lincoln said, "I have never known a person who really knew the Bible that did not believe it to be the inspired Word of God." This has also been the author's experience-that people who really know the Bible, believe it. There is

---

[1] All scriptures are quoted from the English Standard Version, Crossway Publishing, Wheaton, Illinois—www.ESV.org

BIBLICAL ARCHAEOLOGY

a remarkable connection between faith and good biblical knowledge.

One of the themes that runs all the way through the Bible is prophecy about Jesus. Jesus said, "... everything written about me in the Law of Moses and the Prophets and the Psalms ..." (Luke 24:44). Fulfilled prophecy is an example that proves beyond any possible doubt that the Bible is an inspired book from God. Archaeology is another of these proofs of the Bible as an inspired book.

Here is a brief survey about the Jesus prophecies:

1. There are about 500 prophecies about Jesus in the Old Testament.

2. 353 of these prophecies are quoted by the New Testament writers.

3. Just what is the significance of this fact? Think for a moment about predicting the future.
   For example, who will become the next president of the United States in the next election? Extend that to 10 years, 50, 500, or 3000 years. Where will they be born, what will they do in life, and when will they die? It is totally impossible for humans to predict such things. We cannot even predict what will happen tomorrow for certain.

4. Josh McDowell, in his book,[2] quotes a mathematician in regard to the probability of such prophecies being made and then being fulfilled. This expert says that if eight prophecies about Jesus, that were given from 400 to

---

[2] Josh McDowell, *Evidence That Demands a Verdict*, Pages 175-176, Campus Crusade International, Arrowhead Springs, San Bernadino, CA, 1972

3,000 years before his birth, came true, the mathematical probability would be 1 followed by 47 zeros.

Remember how many one trillion is. One trillion seconds is over 33,000 years. Forty-seven zeros is a number so large that there is no name for it, way beyond a trillion.

If we had that number of silver dollars it would cover the state of Texas two feet deep. If only one of these dollars was painted red and a person parachuted out of an airplane 10,000 feet above ground level, blindfolded, and at random could pick up only one coin, his chances would be 1 followed by 47 zeros. There is no chance in an eternity that this would happen.

McDowell's friend then considered the likelihood of 30 prophecies being fulfilled. This number is 1 followed by 157 zeros. Taking our silver dollars example again, if we had this many they would fill up the whole known universe and beyond. But there are not just 30—there are more than 500 prophecies with 7,000-plus references to Jesus if noting the times the word Jehovah is used in the Hebrew text. How could this happen without inspiration?

5. What is being said? An examination of the Bible, without prejudice, will lead to faith. To examine it and not believe it is to demonstrate lack of intelligence, or a carnal, stubborn, and sinful heart.

6. Prophecy is just one of the evidences for the inspiration of the Bible. There are many more ways to demonstrate that the Bible has to be a book from God. Yes, the Bible and salvation were planned by God before the universe was created. "Forever, O LORD, your word is firmly fixed in the heavens" (Psalm 119:89). For certain the Bible is the written Word of Jesus Christ, the living Word. This is the premise this book is founded upon.

BIBLICAL ARCHAEOLOGY

As Dinesh D'Souza says, "The objections to the Bible are not intellectual, but moral."[3] It is the truth. People want to do as they please, not as God directs. The result is the same in the end, sin and death.

WHAT IS THE PURPOSE OF STUDYING BIBLICAL ARCHAEOLOGY?

This study's purpose is not to prove the major claims of the Bible. These claims have already been proven many times and in many ways. Our purpose is different since there is no way that archaeology can prove that God spoke to Moses nor that God sent Nebuchadnezzar to destroy Jerusalem. That is a different field of study.

This study seeks to show that the Bible is historically accurate, that the events recorded in the Bible really happened, and that the Bible talks about real people, kingdoms, and events. In fact, there is archaeological information found throughout the Bible. This evidence is so voluminous as to be astounding. Detail after detail has been substantiated by archaeology.

Gonzalo Baez-Camargo's book, *Archaeological Commentary on the Bible*,[4] shows that the archaeologist's spade has confirmed event after event from Genesis through Revelation. Detail after detail has been substantiated. It is amazing how much archaeological evidence there is for the Bible.

---

3 From a speech given at Eagle Christian Church, Eagle, Idaho

4 Gonzalo, Baez-Camargo, *From Genesis to Revelation. Archaeological Commentary on the Bible*, American Bible Society, Doubleday and Company, Inc. Garden City, New York 1984.

Another supposed Scripture, the Book of Mormon, has little or no archaeological proof. The Bible has maps in the back of it to show the location of places mentioned. The Book of Mormon has no maps, because many of the places mentioned cannot be found. No coins, cities, temples, or battle fields have been found to prove the text. Not all claimed scripture has been proven like the Bible has.

Jesus said in Luke 19:40 when the Jews tried to silence those who were praising Him, "I tell you, if these become silent the stones will cry out!" And this is exactly what has happened. When the unbelieving critics of the Bible were having their heyday trying to destroy the Bible, the archaeologists began to dig, and event after event recorded in the Bible was confirmed.

In 1956, when the author began to study theology, it was said that all but 99 serious problems in the biblical text had been answered. A few years later this number had shrunk to 50, then 30 and now there remain only a very few. Time after time the biblical record has been vindicated. Today, criticizing the Bible and trying to disprove it is left to a few people who are not aware of all that has been done to show the Bible's accuracy.

BIBLICAL ARCHAEOLOGY

The study of Biblical Archaeology came relatively late to Christianity and the Bible. Its beginning seems almost accidental.

Throughout the seventeenth and eighteenth centuries wealthy, adventurous young men travelled to Italy, Greece, and Turkey, exploring, writing descriptions of what they saw, and collecting artifacts from the remains of Greek and Roman civilization.

BIBLICAL ARCHAEOLOGY

As time passed a few went farther on to Syria and Palestine. There they found the spectacular ruins of Baalbeck, Palmyra, Petra, and Roman cities patterned after Greek architecture.

Of course pilgrims had been visiting the holy places for hundreds of years, clear back to Helena (4th century A.D.), mother of Emperor Constantine. But few had taken interest in them as historical or archaeological sites, or studied the visible or covered ruins.

Ancient Egypt had drawn a few adventurers who brought back accounts of the enormous temples, painted tombs, and the pyramids. Early explorations produced some invalid ideas.

Strange explanations of the pyramids were offered. Some had thought they could tell the future by studying them. (They called themselves "British Israelites.") They taught that England and the United States were the lost ten tribes of Israel. They measured the Pyramids with a rubber tape measure that they could stretch to match their preconceived notions of times and events. This illustrates that not everything deduced by these early explorers was valid.

With the beginning of the nineteenth century, a new era dawned in the study of the ancient world. The study began with classical Greece, Assyria, Babylon, and Egypt. It was not until an inscription was found that told of an Old Testament king named Sargon, that interest in this study expanded to a much wider audience.

Soon books were being written to talk of the new discoveries relative to the Bible, and Biblical Archaeology was born. Names that had been almost meaningless in the Bible became real, when it was learned they were real people. The Assyrian tyrants actually appeared, carved on palace walls, with their armies and miserable captives. The great kings of Persia spoke through their own writings, and the Pharaohs of Egypt could be identified.

This was the same period when the Old Testament was being attacked by unbelieving scholars. These unbelievers were denying what the Old Testament books said. They tried to say Abraham lived much later than was said in the Bible text. They affirmed that Moses was not a real person, but grew up as a legend, through the Jewish Priests. Archaeology began to show the Bible's accuracy again and again. The neo-orthodox scholars, as they were called, had egg on their faces and their works were disproven time after time.

Archaeology is most helpful with questions of human history and customs. The archaeologist's spade has shown that the Bible's people were real, the events real, the patterns of behavior described were real, and the Bible has been shown to be an accurate record of what happened.

The archaeologists have helped place the ancient records in their true settings. Rare discoveries, relating directly to passages in the Old and New Testament, time after time have given credibility to these passages. We will be looking at a few of the most notable that help us trace the families of man.

PEOPLE WHO BEGAN THIS WORK

The name Babylon (Babel) has had a mystic aura about it almost forever. Babylon stood for luxury and evil living. Even in the Bible book of Revelation it is the picture of the evils of human wickedness. For centuries no one really knew much about it. A few Europeans visited Baghdad and saw the dusty mounds and picked up bricks with strange writing on them that no one could read.

BIBLICAL ARCHAEOLOGY

The first person to survey and describe the ruins was a remarkable young man, Claudius James Rich. At twenty he arrived in Bombay, India to work for the British East India Company. He had traveled in Turkey, Egypt, and the Near East. He spoke French, Italian, Turkish, Arabic, Persian, and could read Hebrew, Syriac, and some Chinese.

He was assigned to Baghdad in 1807, and in 1811 he took his new 18-year-old bride there with him. They made an excursion to Babylon and Rich toured the mounds, making sketches and rough plans, and setting men to dig for inscribed bricks, seals, and other objects. Rich published this work and a second edition of it later.

Two years later the Riches visited Mosul, the chief city of northern Iraq. From there they visited Nineveh, where he collected bricks and clay tablets. Unfortunately in Persepolis he contacted cholera and died at age thirty-four. He could be said to have been the father of Mesopotamian archaeology. His books were widely read.

Next came Paul Emile Botta, who was sent to Mosul and opened his first trenches in the ruins of Nineveh in December 1842. He found very little in the six weeks he was there. He tried digging at Khorsabad in 1845. Only a little below the ground he found the walls of a great palace, stones carved with pictures, and cuneiform writing. He sent these to Paris where they caused a sensation. Public interest rose higher when it was learned the palace belonged to Sargon, the king of Assyria named in Isaiah 20:1. Archaeology in the region was now on its way.

Next in line came Austen Henry Layard, who dug into the mound called Nimrud and was convinced he had found Nineveh. He wrote a best-selling book about this work. In 1849-1851 they uncovered the palace of Sennacherib, king of Assyria, from 705-681 B.C. In one small room they found thousands of clay cuneiform tablets. He finished his work in 1851.

One scholar, George Smithy, was studying the clay tablets Layard had found and discovered the story of a great flood very similar to the story of Noah's great flood in Genesis. People were learning that there were great treasures to be gained from the dirt, bricks, rocks, and broken pottery.

NOW WE COME TO THE PRIMARY LANDS OF THE BIBLE

Edward Robinson saw the many mounds in Palestine that we now call "tels" (sometimes spelled "tells") and thought they were natural hills. In 1848-1852 he and his friend Eli Smith explored the land and identified 100 places named in the Bible. Their research was published in a book called *Biblical Researches in Palestine*, 1856.

Another American, W. F. Lynch, fabricated a metal boat and floated the Jordan from Galilee to the Dead Sea. This took a week and they discovered that the Dead Sea was 1,300 feet below sea level.

Between 1872 and 1878, C. R. Conder and H. H. Kitchener surveyed the country, marking over 10,000 sites. Their work still underlies modern maps.

It was Flinders Petrie who discovered that pottery from different levels could help in dating the periods. Pottery, like modern car styles, changed year by year and the styles were similar throughout an area. He could tell which pieces were the oldest and which were newer to classify their age. This method is still used in dating archaeological sites. Other artifacts and inscriptions, as well as Carbon 14 dating helped determine the dates of what was being excavated. (More will be said about this later.)

W. F. Albright began to excavate in 1922 and refined the process of dating using pottery, comparing pottery from multiple sites.

Dame Kathleen Kenyon (1906–1978) was one of the most influential of the early archaeologists. She made extensive excavations at Jericho (1952–1958). She followed the excavation plan she had learned from Mortimer Wheeler.

DATING OF ARCHAEOLOGICAL SITES

Several different methods are used to date the time period of what is excavated. One of the earliest, as already stated, is the use of pottery.

One archaeologist said, "It appears that half of the ancient world was making pottery and the other half breaking it." This in part explains the growth of the tels. Earthquakes, wars, and accumulation of rubbish caused one layer to be built upon another.

Another way of dating is coinage, or items of financial exchange. This is easier in the later periods in the Bible from 400 B.C. and forward, as coins were in common use. Earlier there were other items of financial exchange.

Inscriptions on clay tablets help to date the periods. Clay was readily available and with a stylus one could write on them and if it was important, sun dry, or fire them, to make a permanent record. Other more important things were inscribed on metal or stone.

More recently, Carbon 14 dating has helped to determine the age of archaeological items found.

CARBON 14 DATING

1. Carbon 14 is a carbon element that is unstable. Living things accumulate Carbon 14 while living and when they die it begins to dissipate at a predictable rate.

2. It comes from the upper atmosphere and sun and affects all living things.

3. Plants, animals, living, and built things accumulate this during their lives. At death it begins to dissipate. It is minimally radioactive.

4. The things that are dateable are charcoal, wood, twigs, seeds, bones, shells, peat, hair, pottery, pollen, paintings, coral, fabrics, paper, parchment, resins, water, and many other things.

5. There is a 10% margin of error.

6. Carbon 14 dating would not be valid before the flood since it is based on uniformity and things were almost certainly atmospherically different before the flood.

SUMMARY

Our study will begin with the flood of Noah and follow Noah and his sons as the families of man developed after the Ark came to rest on Mt. Ararat. There appears to be almost nothing of archaeological discovery about civilization before the time of Noah.

BIBLICAL ARCHAEOLOGY

There is considerable evidence for a worldwide flood. This evidence will be surveyed. Many quality books have been written about this subject and thus we will only give a summary of evidence that supports the biblical account of the Flood.

We will examine the evidence for Noah's Ark; was it real and is there archaeological evidence for it? Has it been found? The search goes on still today, but a lot of evidence for its existence will be given.

We will turn our attention to a series of connected events beginning with the Tower of Babel, then Ebla and the 16,000-volume library found there from 2200 B.C., on to Ur of the Chaldees, Laish, Tel Dan, Tel Aviv, Sodom and Gomorrah, the Pyramids of Egypt, the Red Sea Crossing, Jericho, Bethel-Gibeon, Megiddo, ancient languages, the Gihon and Warren's Shaft, Nineveh, Babylon, and other places and events.

Suggested Reading:[5]
McDowell, Josh; *Evidence that Demands a Verdict*.
Gonzalo, Baez: *Archaeological Commentary on the Bible*.

---

5 See bibliography for details about the suggested reading books.

Chapter Two

The Flood of Noah

Let us begin our study of archaeology with the flood of Noah and trace the families of mankind from there until modern times.

Although some may not agree, yet it is true, archaeological discovery begins shortly after the flood of Noah, not before. The author's research has found no pre-flood cities, graveyards or signs of civilization.

If one does not accept the historical event of the flood, it leaves a most puzzling dilemma—what happened to civilization before the flood? Yes, it is true that some creatures' remains have been found, but commonly they are encased in water-laid clay or under tons of debris, which adds credence to the flood account.

Beginning with the Flood, we will take up our study with the Tower of Babel and Noah and his sons. We will follow the families of man using archaeology and the Bible histories, comparing them to document biblical accuracy.

The goal will be to not only demonstrate biblical accuracy but to show that humanity today can trace their lineage back to Noah or one of his sons.

BIBLICAL ARCHAEOLOGY

This study will begin with Genesis chapters seven and eight and which describe the great worldwide Flood of Noah. Most ancient histories of the nations of the world have flood accounts. More than 300 of these flood accounts have been found. The versions vary, but this common thread through all civilizations illustrate that there certainly was some event that has been carried on in each nation's folklore and history.[6]

The Bible tells us that there were two things that happened to bring about the flood—one came from the sky and the other came from the earth. Genesis 7:11 says, "In the six hundredth year of Noah's life, in the second month, on the seventeenth day of the month, on that day all the fountains of the great deep burst forth, and the windows of the heavens were opened."

The Hebrew word used here for "burst forth" is *niphal*, third person plural, and the basic meaning is that the earth "was opened, was cleft, divided itself, was cleaved, broken open or rent." This is saying that the earth was broken up and destroyed. The word is plural, meaning that this rending of the earth happened over and over, repeatedly, multiple times. When it says that the fountains of the deep were opened it tells us that the water in the earth was brought forth. All major water sources were brought to the earth's surface and the earth suffered a massive flood and major changes.

At the same time the water that formed the vapor shield that had surrounded the earth was removed from the sky and fell on the earth. This would bring a major change to temperatures on the earth, as is true on a clear night, in comparison to a cloudy one. The change in temperature would be most drastic at the earth's poles and near the equator. The point

---

6   See the book *In Search of Noah's Ark*, Balsiger & Sellier.

being made is that the earth and atmosphere were drastically changed.

Now let us turn our attention to when this took place. According to Sebastian Adams, well-known world historian, this flood took place about 2348 B.C.[7] The exact date is open to discussion and might have been earlier, but probably not later. There is room for discussion about the date.

Many honest seekers after truth have debated issues about the Flood, and it is not our purpose to question the faith or honesty of those with differing viewpoints, but to do our best to ascertain what really happened. Even though you might not agree with all points being made about the flood, it is our hope that the overall picture will still be clear—that world history can best be understood by believing there was a worldwide flood. Beginning with the Flood, mankind's existence on the earth can be traced, as well as how people were spread over the earth from the Tower of Babel not too long thereafter.

Often scientists and theologians have not been conversant in the others' field of study. This has sometimes led to unnecessary controversy between these two groups.

There is compelling evidence for a worldwide flood. There are two routes that could be followed to prove this affirmation. One is the scientific, and the other, what is apparent to the average person who has not had the training of the scientist. The latter is found by observation. Our approach will be the latter with a smattering of the scientific. Are there observable things that suggest a worldwide flood? The answer is yes.

---

7   See *Adams' SynChronological Chart or Map of History*.

BIBLICAL ARCHAEOLOGY

The inspiration and accuracy of the Bible is not under discussion here; the Bible has already been proven. The purpose here is to add another layer of physical evidence to the already existent material proving the inspiration of the Bible.

We are not questioning the inspiration of the Bible or doubting the history given by Moses. But we will be observing additional evidence for the flood. In this study we are looking for physical evidence for the flood and the origin of the families of man.

The goal is to establish the historical truthfulness of the Flood and beginning upon this foundation to trace humanity on the earth. It is affirmed that the existing families of mankind have their roots in Noah's family—Shem, Ham and Japheth. Did the Flood really happen? If so, can we learn about modern civilization's lineage back to that event?

EVIDENCE FOR A WORLDWIDE FLOOD

First, let us look at several small pieces of physical evidence that suggest that there has been such an event as a worldwide flood.

1. The author's father, Claude C. Crane, spent his whole life working as a road builder. He helped build Highway 20 across the Cascade Mountains of Oregon. While excavating for the road bed, about 4,000 feet above sea level, he found a petrified clam in the excavation. The author has this petrified clam. How did this ocean creature get buried high in the Cascade Mountains?

2. From the time he was a boy Claude was interested in rocks. He was hiking on a butte near Lebanon, Oregon, and near the top of this butte found another petrified clam. Interesting to our discussion is how this clam got into a gravel bed near the top of this high butte.

3. In 1970 the author was living in Salt Lake City, Utah. Salt Lake City is surrounded by mountains. To the east are the Wasatch Mountains and the west are the Oquirrh Mountains. Some of the highest peaks are over 13,000 feet high. He decided to climb the Wasatch Mountains. He noticed that as one climbed there were rings around the mountains east and west that looked very much like the shoreline of a vast lake. As far as one looks around these mountains there are these shoreline markings, symmetrical all the way around. When was this area covered by water, leaving this receding shoreline? There is pretty clear evidence that these mountains were water covered at one time.

4. Stand and look at the Grand Canyon and ask yourself, when was there water enough to cut this mighty gorge?

5. If traveling in Utah, take time to stop and look at the dinosaur beds. These large reptile remains were buried in water-laid clay that hardened into rock. What drowned these huge creatures and buried them? What caused all the muck that buried their remains? It looks like there was a massive flood here sometime, since these creatures are so high above the elevation of any sea.

6. In the author's personal collection is a mammoth tusk that was found in the permafrost of Alaska (see picture). Along with it is a piece of petrified whale bone. In Alaska and Siberia there are large deposits of these mammoths, some with green grass still in their mouths. There are many of these large creatures that were drowned, fast frozen, and buried under flood debris. What scientific explanation can be given for how

they got where they are? How is this explained? Does not a massive cataclysmic event, like the Flood of Noah, make sense?

7. While traveling in Tennessee the author visited a coal miner's museum. The guide said he had spent 35 years working in the coal mines; the last 25 years he was a foreman over several mining operations. He was asked what coal came from. He explained that coal was made up of decomposed animal and plant matter. He showed petrified limbs, stumps, and other forms of life buried in the coal, but the coal itself was animal and plant matter buried together. What had gathered these large deposits of animals and plants together, with existing limbs, stumps, and debris mixed in? Does not reason suggest there must have been some great cataclysmic event?

The guide brought out a piece of shale that was about one inch thick and explained that wherever they found coal it was covered over with shale, and showed that this shale had in it ferns, branches, leaves, and plant life. He said that at some time past, the coal had obviously been buried by a large flood of water and over it was mud containing debris of plant life. When it dried it hardened much like concrete or mortar. The picture here is a piece of this shale that the author has in his collection. The leaves and plant life are clearly visible. The guide said that no doubt coal came from some kind of major catastrophe.

8. What about oil and petroleum deposits? Where did they come from? Now we move from personal, non-scientific observations, to information from men who have given their lives to the study of science and believe in the Genesis flood of Noah. These men are John C. Whitcomb Jr., Th.D; Henry M. Morris, Ph.D; and John C. McCampbell, Ph.D. One is a doctor of theology and the others eminent scientists. It is not the purpose of this study to discuss all the scientific material that can be given for the flood, but to summarize, briefly, enough information to establish that the flood really happened. Two of the above named men wrote a book, *The Genesis Flood, the Biblical Record and Its Scientific Implications*.[8] This book is over 500 pages long and a classic work showing that the flood really happened. These are highly trained men who are specialists in their field. In their book they present the evidence for a worldwide flood and answer most, if not all, of the objections to the flood.

It is our thesis that petroleum products and coal each are a by-product of the flood of Noah. Regarding the oil deposits, they say:

"The Formation of Petroleum Deposits"

"The most immediately apparent conclusion from all this is that the accumulation of petroleum into traps must have occurred after all, or practically all, the strata were laid down, since they are apparently entirely independent of the particular type of rock but are, nevertheless, similar to each other in hydraulic characteristics. The main feature that all such deposits have in common is that of being associated with water:

---

8 *The Genesis Flood*, John C. Whitcomb, Jr. & Henry M. Morris.

BIBLICAL ARCHAEOLOGY

Nearly every petroleum pool exists within an environment of water—free, interstitial, edge, and bottom water. This means that the problem of migration is intimately related to hydrology, hydraulics, and ground-water movement.

Another extremely important fact is that apparently all petroleum is organic in origin. There have been inorganic theories of origin in the past, but the accumulated evidence now is overwhelming that petroleum has an organic basis ... .

Although the details are not clear, the Deluge once again appears to offer a satisfactory explanation for the origin of oil, as well as the other stratigraphic phenomena. The great sedimentary basins being filled rapidly and more or less continuously during the Flood would provide a prolific source of organic material, together with whatever heat and pressure might have been needed to initiate the chemical reactions necessary to begin the transformation into petroleum hydro-carbons. Of course, not all organic debris deposited during the Flood was converted into oil ... .

Thus, it would seem that crude oil originates during the compaction of a sedimentary basin by virtue of the fact that sediment hydrocarbons dissolve in water containing natural solubilizers and then come out of solution as oil droplets ... ."[9]

It is commonly believed that coal and petroleum products primarily have an animal and plant life origin. This would necessitate huge amounts of animals and plants to be buried together at one time. They would have to have been buried in basins and covered over with debris

---

9   Ibid, Pages 434-435.

of water-laid items and that could best be explained by a huge worldwide cataclysmic flood.

9. Where did all this organic material come from? There would have to be at least two sources—a large amount of vegetation and huge quantities of animal matter. The Bible gives us clues to both of these sources.

Genesis hints that before the flood things were vastly different than after the flood. Here are a couple of these hints. Genesis 2:6 says, "and a mist was going up from the land and was watering the whole face of the ground." First, it does not say rain, but mist rising from the ground, not falling from the sky. Second, it says "the whole face of the ground." Could not this hint that this was worldwide? This would facilitate a warmer climate worldwide and lush vegetation wherever there was land.

The next hint is that before the flood there had not been rainbows. Genesis 9:13–14—"I have set my bow in the cloud, and it shall be a sign of the covenant between me and the earth when I bring clouds over the earth and the bow is seen in the clouds, ..." Rainbows are caused by sunlight shining through water vapor. If the earth had been covered with a mist and vapor there would have been no rainbows and it would have produced much more vegetation. The study of geology seems to indicate that at one time the earth was covered from pole to pole with vegetation.

The other comment is about clouds. Before this there is no mention of clouds. It appears that there was a change in how the earth was going to operate. This would explain the large amounts of vegetation required for all this oil and coal creation.

But where did all the animal life come from? With all this vegetation it would be understandable that animals would have proliferated, including many which did not survive the flood because they did not find their way into the Ark. There is plentiful evidence of the many creatures that used to be on the earth and no longer exist. Their existence is shown by their remains being found buried in water-laid clay and debris and in the permafrost of Alaska and Siberia.

POPULATION ON THE EARTH IN NOAH'S DAY

What would the population of humans have been on the earth by the time of Noah? By the Flood's time the earth's human population would have been enormous, possibly as many as 4–5 billion or more people. At first glance this seems improbable, but let us not be too hasty in drawing a conclusion.

Henry Morris' book, *Biblical Cosmology and Modern Science*, discusses the earth's probable population by Noah's time and I quote: "A remarkable commentary on human history is the fact that man as a whole has broken all of God's commandments except the very first. Immediately after the creation of man, God said to him: 'Be fruitful and multiply and fill the earth'" (Genesis 1:28).

The population explosion of modern times points to an earlier time when the earth was also covered with people. Morris quotes from Genesis 6:11: "... and the earth was filled with violence ..." It says the same thing again in verse 13. This suggests that people filled the earth.

Some have been skeptical that the earth's population could have grown so rapidly in the 1,656 or more years before the Flood. It is helpful to calculate just what this population could have become.

Jewish tradition speculates that Adam and Eve could have had as many as 50–60 children. The question, "Where did Cain get

DR. CHARLES CRANE

his wife?" is often asked, and the answer is that he must have married a sister and with that many children there would have been several possible wives he could have chosen.

As a boy I was asked whether I would rather be paid $1,000 for a month's work (a huge sum for that time) or 1 cent a day doubled each day for thirty days. At first thought the $1,000 seemed the best choice, but the person asked me to figure it out. Those who have tried this experiment know what a mistake it would have been to take the $1,000. On the 27th day doubling the penny would be $67,108,864.00. Such is the case with the growth of population.

Morris gives a chart to illustrate population growth:

5 generations, population	96 people
10 generations, population	3,070 people
15 generations, population	98,300 people
20 generations, population	3,150,000 people
30 generations, population	3,220,000,000 people [10]

This would mean that in the time from creation until the Flood, the population could have been as much as four to five billion people. It is astounding, but true. The earth was filled with people and violence.

Imagine what the animal population must have been to provide for all of these people and to fill the fields and forests of the earth. What happened to all these animals and people? If mankind had been on the earth for 500,000 years or more, as suggested by the evolutionists, there would not have been standing room for all of them, but they would have been shoulder to shoulder from South to North Pole covering the whole earth.

---

[10] Henry Morris, *Biblical Cosmology and Modern Science*. Morris, page 74.

BIBLICAL ARCHAEOLOGY

Another factor to suggest the gigantic population numbers is that people lived much longer before the flood. Their longer life spans could be explained because the vapor barrier filtered out the harmful radiation rays of the sun and thus extended their lifespans.

Where are all the graveyards for these pre-flood people? Where are their cities? Why then after Babel do we find the growth of civilization, established and documented, but nothing but coal and oil, before the flood?

Is it not reasonable to think that there was some huge catastrophe to wipe them out and bury them and their flocks in mass watery graves and cover them over with the muck, residue and debris from the Flood? The Flood would have washed them to the lowest spot or valley and covered them over with debris. And this is just what we find, large deposits and pools of coal and petroleum gathered in basins and covered with debris.

With such a large population of people and animals gathered into cities, and in valleys, when they were drowned they would have floated together at the lowest elevation and been covered with the deposits of debris created by the massive storm, rain and flood and the upheaval of the earth. People would have flocked together and suffered their terrible doom, resulting in what we now call coal and oil, which are in reality the remains of the massive population of sinners, vegetation and animals. It is sobering to think that when a person drives their automobile, it may be fueled by the remains of some old sinner who was drowned in the flood.[11]

---

11 For further information on this subject, see *Biblical Cosmology and Modern Science* by Dr. Henry Morris and published by Craig Press, Nutley, New Jersey, 1970.

DR. CHARLES CRANE

A substantial library of books has been written on this subject, but our purpose here is to point out that believing in the flood of Noah is reasonable. There are thousands of qualified scientists and theologians who accept the world wide flood as a historical fact. Accepting the Flood of Noah as an historical fact answers a host of problems for which the secular scientist struggles to find answers.

Suggested Reading:
Balsiger, Dave and Sellier, Charles E. Jr., *In Search of Noah's Ark*.
Morris and Whitcomb, *The Genesis Flood*.
Morris, *Biblical Cosmology and Modern Science*.

Chapter Three

Noah's Ark

Was there an ark? Did Noah build it? Was it adequate to carry all known air-breathing species through an extended flood to safety? These and related questions will be the subjects of this chapter.

According to Genesis 6:14-17, Noah was told to build an ark:

> Make yourself an ark of gopher wood. Make rooms in the ark, and cover it inside and out with pitch. This is how you are to make it: the length of the ark 300 cubits, its breadth 50 cubits, and its height 30 cubits. Make a roof for the ark, and finish it to a cubit above, and set the door of the ark in its side. Make it with lower, second and third decks. For behold, I will bring a flood of waters upon the earth to destroy all flesh in which is the breath of life under heaven.

A cubit was 18–22 inches, the distance from a man's elbow to the tip of his fingers. This would mean that the Ark was from 450-525 feet long, 75–87.5 feet wide and 45–52.5 feet high. The smaller measure would mean the inside size would be the same as 503 giant railroad boxcars, weighing 81,000 tons or 162,000,000 pounds. It would have been roughly the size of the Battleship Oregon.

DR. CHARLES CRANE

A replica of the Ark has just been finished in Williamstown, Kentucky by Ken Ham. Ham demonstrates that the Ark was big enough to house all of the known air-breathing species. It was more of a barge than a ship. Tests have been taken to see if it was sea worthy and these tests have shown that it could, if built strong enough, withstand the roughest of seas.

It is not our purpose to exhaustively examine the building of the Ark and its construction. (Although those who claim to have seen it say it was built of massive timbers.) Our goal is to see if there is credible archaeological evidence for the Ark's existence and whether its remains still exist on Mt. Ararat today. Probably no other archaeological endeavor has produced such long and passionate efforts by mankind. Books have been written about the Ark, expeditions launched to find it, and movies made about the search for it.[12] [13]

On the very first page of the book *In Search of Noah's Ark* it says:

THE 5,000-YEAR-OLD MYSTERY

> In 1840 there was a violent earthquake in Eastern Turkey. An expedition checking for damage discovered a gigantic wooden ship high atop Mt. Ararat.
>
> In 1876, British statesman Sir James Bryce climbed Mt. Ararat alone and returned with a five-foot piece of hand-hewn timber.

---

12 Balsinger and Sellier's book is called *In Search of Noah's Ark* and it was made into a movie.

13 Balsinger and Sellier, Sun Classic Books, L.A. California, 1976.

BIBLICAL ARCHAEOLOGY

In 1887, Prince John Joseph Nouri ascended Mt. Ararat and found a vessel with stalls and cages on board.

In 1955, French engineer Fernand Navarra brought back the first photographs of the mysterious ship. Some have questioned Navarra's findings, but considered along with so many other witnesses it is possible that his findings are authentic.

In 1972, an earth resources satellite was launched 450 miles above Earth. As it passed over the Turkish-Russian border it recorded a mysterious boat-like object on Mt. Ararat.

Where did this mysterious ship come from?
Who put it there?
What was its cargo?[14]

This is from just one of the many books about Noah's Ark. Some are fanciful and not of great value. But other books give information that is quite convincing that the Ark's remains are still encased in a permanent glacier high on Mt. Ararat in Turkey.

EVIDENCE FOR THE ARK'S EXISTENCE

Just what is the evidence for the existence of the Ark?

- The Bible has been proven to be historically accurate every place that it can be checked.

- The Great Flood is found mentioned in the history of most cultures—Greece, India, and even among Native

---

14 *In Search of Noah's Ark*, Balsiger and Sellier, Jr. The first page.

Americans. In each of these reports, the Ark lands on a mountain top.

- There are many and varied people, who have for over 1,000 years, claimed to have seen the remains of the Ark. Most are people of unimpeachable character.

- Those who claim to have seen it give very similar descriptions of what they saw.

- More than one witness has brought back a chunk of wood from it that in each case, when tested, has shown that the wood was very old, possibly as much as 5,000 years old.

As we contemplate the existence of the Ark, here are the indisputable facts:

1. Many witnesses say that at about 14,000 feet on Mt. Ararat, in Turkey, there is a large wooden boat-like structure buried many feet deep in the ice.

2. A boat-like structure has been mentioned as being on Mt. Ararat by explorers and historians as early as 700 B.C.

3. During the 1800s this structure was observed by many local explorers including military authorities who gave it official government recognition in the news media.

4. In 1955, a filmed expedition recovered wood from the structure about 35 feet below the ice's surface.

5. The recovered wood, subjected to testing for dating, was thought to be from 1,500–5,000 years old.

BIBLICAL ARCHAEOLOGY

6. In the decade of the 1970s, American spy planes and military satellite photos show the Ark on Mt. Ararat.

7. The only reliable historical source that can be used to identify the origin of this large wood item is the Bible.[15]

8. Then there are the many Bible passages and people that mention Noah's Ark:

   a) Genesis 6—7
   b) Isaiah 54:9
   c) Ezekiel 14:14 & 20
   d) Matthew 24:37
   e) Luke 3:36 & 17:26
   f) Hebrews 11:7
   g) I Peter 3:20
   h) II Peter 2:5

   This means that Moses, Isaiah, Ezekiel, Jesus, Matthew, Luke, Paul, and Peter believed in the flood of Noah and there being a Noah's Ark.

9. A 2010 Chinese expedition to find the Ark claimed they did find it. It was buried deep in the ice and they got to it by descending about 50 feet through a crevasse in the ice and were able to enter it. They took pictures of the crevasse and inside the ark, and described how it was constructed. They reported that it had more than one story, had rooms, and stalls inside. They found remnants of frozen grain, straw, rope, and brought back some of these items. The wood they brought back tested to be 4,800 years old. They claim that they are 99.9% sure the wood they brought back was from Noah's Ark.

---

15 Ibid, pgs 2-3.

This area of Turkey is very dangerous for foreigners to enter today. It is a military area and also infested with thieves and robbers. It is a war-torn place, and because of Islam's influence Christians are especially unwelcome.

There are many other historical accounts that have been found about the flood of Noah. The Sumerian Tablets, Babylonian records, and the Ebla Tablets all make reference to a great flood. Some of these records date back as far as 2000 B.C., which would be just a few hundred years after the event took place.

King Asharbanipal mentions a great flood and wrote about it on clay tablets. Among these tablets was found the Gilgamesh Epic that talks about the Flood.

10. Many well-know people have talked about the Ark throughout History.

 a) John Chrysostom (A.D. 345–407) the patriarch of Constantinople who was considered to be the greatest preacher of his time said, "Let us therefore ask them (the unbelieving): Have you heard of the Flood—of that universal destruction? That was not just a threat, was it? Did it not really come to pass—was not this mighty work carried out? Do not the mountains of Armenia testify to it, where the Ark rested? And are not the remains of the Ark preserved there to this very day for an admonition?"[16]

 b) Epiphanius of Salamis (A.D. 315–403) was a Palestine born monk and Bishop of Constantia, and wrote about the Ark: "Do you seriously suppose that we were unable to prove our point, when even to this day the remains of Noah's Ark are shown in the country of the Kurds? Why,

---

[16] Ibid, pg 76.

were one to search diligently, doubtless one would also find at the foot of the mountain the remnants of the altar where Noah, on leaving the Ark, tarried to offer clean and fatty animals as a sacrifice to the Lord God."[17]

c) Marco Polo (A.D. 1234–1324), the renowned explorer, says in his book *The Travels*: "And you should know that in this land of Armenia, the Ark of Noah still rests on top of a certain great mountain where the snow stays so long that no one can climb it. The snow never melts—it gets thicker with each snowfall."[18]

d) Jehan Haithon, an Armenian Prince of the 13th Century, wrote, "In Armenia there is a very high mountain ... and its name is Ararat. On that mountain Noah's Ark landed after the Flood ... at the summit a great black object is always visible, which is said to be the Ark of Noah."[19]

e) Vincent Beauvais (1256), said, "In Armenia there is a noble city called Ani where a thousand churches and a hundred thousand families or households are to be found ... Near it is Mount Ararat, where Noah's Ark rests, and at the foot of that mountain is the first city which Noah built, was called Laudume."[20]

f) Jans Janszoom Struys, of the 17th Century, tells about a monk he went to treat for a hernia near Ararat. The monk was so thankful he gave him a cross made out of wood from Noah's Ark.[21]

---

17 Ibid, pg 77.

18 Ibid, pg 77.

19 Ibid, pg 77.

20 Ibid, pg 78.

21 A summary of material from *In Search of Noah's Ark*.

Not all ancient accounts report that there was an actual Noah's Ark on Mt. Ararat. Yet, there are so many very credible people, over such a long period of time, each telling a similar story of its existence and so many of these claim to have seen it, that the evidence is pretty impressive.

We now have sufficient information to proceed with our study. We have begun with the great flood and Noah's Ark. Our goal now is to trace the history of mankind from Noah and his three sons, Shem, Ham and Japheth, archaeologically. We will primarily follow the biblical narrative.

Genesis 10 tells about the children of Noah and their families and where they settled. It does not tell where Noah settled. Noah lived another 350 years after the flood. The most ancient histories point to China as the place where Noah settled. The ancient Chinese histories claim Oah or Foah, who came from the great flood, was their founding ancestor.

> Suggested Reading:
> Genesis 6:9—8:22
> Adams, Sebastian, *Synchronological Chart of World History*.

Chapter Four

The Tower of Babel

Genesis 11:1–9

TWO IMPORTANT THINGS

This passage of scripture explains two things about the history of humanity. First, how the many diverse languages came to be, and the second is how people groups were spread over the earth after the Flood. It is an interesting story, but does it have archaeological proof? The answer to this question is yes.

Before the Flood, the population of the world was great. Considering the time span and that people lived much longer then than now, it is estimated that before the flood the population of the earth was thought to be from 4–5 billion. This was covered in Chapter Two.

After the Flood, the human race was young and had been purified by the Flood to a single godly family. Many diseases and genetic damages were not present that entered the race over time. People lived longer than they do today. During the 101 years after the Flood and the tower of Babel, population growth would have been substantial, as already illustrated.

THE TOWER OF BABEL

The Tower of Babel came four or five generations after the end of the Flood, or 101 years later, 1,656 years after Eden, about 2348–2500 B.C. Historians do not agree about these dates, but this appears to be a reasonable suggestion. The time between the Flood and Babel could have been somewhat longer.

The large population is explained in that women could have babies every 15–20 months and that these children could begin to procreate at or before age 20, and that for some time after the Flood, people lived several hundred years. This explains why the population would have grown so rapidly on the earth before the Flood.

The grand structure reaching into heaven seems to have originated at a place that later came to be known as Babylon. The Bible calls this huge structure "The Tower of Babel." The name Babel comes from the Hebrew word, Balol, which means to confound, which is what God did to their common language at Babel. Even today we speak of someone who is not talking coherently as "babbling."

God commanded them to multiply and fill the earth. They decided they did not want to do this and were building a tower to heaven to keep them from being spread across the earth.

Thus the root of the name Babylon comes from confound. That Babylon still exists is evidence that something happened here that confounded people. This ancient city is the first mentioned after the great flood of Noah.

One of the earliest extra-biblical accounts of the Tower of Babel is given by Herodotus in 440 B.C. He claimed to have seen it. This was 1,900 years after the event, yet about 2,450 years closer to the event than we are, and at that time more evidence would have remained of the tower than today. Herodotus is said to be the father of historians, which would be true if we are speaking of secular historians.

The Egyptian Pyramids are only somewhat younger than the Tower of Babel. Herodotus says that the Tower of Babel was 650 feet high and one quarter mile square. He said there was a stairway that wound around it that led to the top of the eight stories. These stories would have been much taller than ours.

These ancient towers were later called "ziggurats," but the Hebrews did not have this word in their vocabulary so they used the word "tower." These ziggurats spread through the ancient world and about 30 have been found in Mesopotamia. They have been found as far south as Ur, at Babylon, and north as far as Tel Brek.

These ziggurats have stairs or ramps for people to ascend to the tops, where temples were common. They were thought to be a "resting place for the gods" or ladders to god and became places for temples to be built for the worship of pagan gods.

This story of the Tower of Babel is certainly true as it is based on a common practice found during this period and throughout this region. This practice of building ziggurats almost certainly had its origin at Babylon some 101 or more years after Noah and his family left the ark.

At that time Noah's family had not yet been spread over the earth. Genesis 9—10 tells us of Noah's children and grandchildren. Chapter 11 explains how and where they were scattered over the earth.

The tower was stopped by the confusion of tongues and possibly finished later and was maintained for many years thereafter as a part of the grand city of Babylon. It probably became the center around which the city of Babylon was built.

Towers like this became popular and graced surrounding cities, several cities thinking they needed a ziggurat since the queen city of the earth had one. Some of these towers have been identified as the original Tower of Babel, but they are not.

The Tower of Babel may have been the influence behind the great Pyramids of Egypt that came 250–300 years later. The oldest large pyramid in Egypt is built in a similar shape to the ziggurats. The author has seen it many times.

Other towers and massive tombs have been found but were of a later date. (Dates: The Tower of Babel, 2248 B.C., and the pyramids began to be built 1950 B.C. and grew more massive in the following years.) There are more than 130 pyramids that have been found in Egypt today. Ground penetrating radar has been utilized to augment the search.

As was said earlier, the Tower of Babel was reported to have been 650 feet tall, while the Cheops Pyramid, the largest, is 476 feet and Cephron, the second largest Pyramid, is 461 feet tall. The Sphinx predates the Pyramids of Giza. These massive structures were built with an effort to bring immortality to the pharaohs buried there. We learn from the contents of King Tut's tomb that everything needed in a future life was buried with them.

Another word about Babylon is in order. For 1,700 years she was the queen city of the whole world, and her beginning was built around a monument in a bogus attempt to find God. They thought that mankind, by their own effort, could build

BIBLICAL ARCHAEOLOGY

a tower that would get them to heaven. Some today are still trying to build their own route to heaven.

Let us take a look at the traditional site in comparison to the real site of the tower. As has already been said, some of the copies of Babel have been supposed to be the real one. Early archaeologists thought other places fit the biblical spot. Most today believe that this site had to be in or near Babylon. The actual site is today a big hole in the ground according to Halley in his handbook. Why?[22]

The Tower of Babel was built of the finest of materials, not sun-dried brick, but fired brick (Genesis 11:3, "make brick and burn them thoroughly"). The mortar was tar, or a petroleum product; the Hebrew word is "bitumen." When the tower fell into disuse and decay, people began to mine the brick for other buildings, homes or businesses. It was a cheap source of material and Babel became a great brick quarry. Since the tower had to have a strong foundation, the bricks went far below the surface of the ground, and hardly anything of this massive structure remains today except a big hole in the ground.

Sir Henry Rawlinson found an inscription about one of these towers that said,

> The tower of Borsippa, which a former king erected and completed to a height of 42 cubits (61 feet), whose summit he did not finish, fell to ruins in ancient times. There was no proper care of its gutters for the water, rain and storms had washed away its brick, and the tiles of its roof were broken. The great god Marduk urged me to restore it. I did not alter its site, or change its foundation walls. At a favorable time I

---

22 *Halley's Handbook*, pg 82.

renewed its brick work and its roofing tiles, and I wrote my name on the cornices of the edifice. I built it anew as it had been ages before; I erected its pinnacle as was in remote days.[23]

This record sounds very much like an unfinished tower that was left and later finished and possibly could have been the Tower of Babel.

Archaeologist G. Smith found an ancient tablet that read, "The building of this illustrious tower offended the gods. In a night they threw down what they had built. They scattered them abroad, and made strange their speech. Their progress they impeded. They wept hot tears for Babylon."[24]

This sounds very much like the biblical account and gives archaeological confirmation of the biblical account.

WHERE WERE THE PEOPLE SCATTERED?

A study of *Sebastian Adam's Chart or Map of History* shows how Noah's family spread across the earth. His chart traces modern races back to their lineage from Noah and his sons. The chart begins with Adam and Eve and concludes with presidents of the United States.

Adams said a picture of history helped his students understand the family of man from beginning to modern times. This chart can be very helpful in explaining the history of the world from a Christian perspective.[25]

---

23 Ibid., pg 82.

24 Ibid., pg 82-83.

25 These charts are available on line or at bookstores. They are reasonably priced.

BIBLICAL ARCHAEOLOGY

It is probable that at the Tower of Babel, Noah's three sons and their children were sent to many different places, 101 or more years after the Flood. Genesis 9–10 tells of Noah's three sons and their children and how they were the basis of all modern races today. This helps us understand where modern races and languages came from.

Shem and family resided in Palestine and the surrounding areas, Japheth went to Europe, Ham to Africa, and Noah to China and the Far East. The oldest Chinese history says their ancestor "Oah," came from the great flood. Noah lived 350 years after the Flood (Genesis 9:28), for a total lifespan of 950 years. He would have had many more children and he became the father of one of the earth's greatest nations today, China.

Finding this much evidence for an account clear back in Genesis 11 helps to illustrate how archaeology has substantiated our Holy Bible. Such evidence is non-existent for other supposed ancient books of scripture and history. Even Herodotus, the father of historians, has often been proven inaccurate in his histories, but not so with our Bible.

We have begun with the oldest event for which archaeologists have found evidence, the flood of Noah, and now to the next great biblical event, the Tower of Babel. Next we will study an event that is almost as important to biblical history as the finding of the Dead Sea Scrolls. This is the discovery of Ebla and its more than 17,000 clay tablets.

The flood was about 2348 B.C., the Tower of Babel 2247 B.C. It is at that time that Ebla comes on the scene. Ebla was most likely founded by those dispersed from Babel that were from the family of Shem and from which also the Hebrews came.

Suggested Reading:

Halley, Henry H., *Halley's Handbook*. (A good handbook of biblical information, a helpful tool in your Christian resource material.)

Chapter Five

Ebla in Syria

ARCHAEOLOGICAL FINDINGS OF GREAT VALUE

The archaeological finds at Ebla are of a similar value to the finding of the Dead Sea Scrolls at Qumran, Israel. More than 17,000 clay tablets have been unearthed at Ebla, and they cover almost all aspects of daily life in the city. They deal with government, commerce, business, education, construction, geography, other kingdoms, and much more. For centuries the city had been lost to civilization and it was almost totally forgotten. It was covered by mounds of sand and dirt and was only recognizable as a large mound in the desert.

EBLA'S LOCATION

Ebla was located in Northern Syria, inland some seventy miles from Antioch of Syria and Seleucia. Although forgotten in modern times, in the past it was, for a time, a center of the ancient world. It was a place of the Hittites and Amorites; the latter were of a similar family tree (Shem) as the Hebrews. Ebla conquered the area called Assyria, Babylon, and controlled as far away as Egypt. For quite a long period they ruled this part of the ancient world.

Ebla was identified in 1968 by Paolo Matthiae of Rome University. The mound or tel, was fifty feet high, covered by sand and dirt blown over by the desert winds.

Today the site is called Tel Madikh. It was destroyed about 2200-2000 B.C. It had been the center of a State that could rival the other cities of Mesopotamia and for a time ruled over them.[26]

MASSIVE LIBRARY FOUND

Archaeologists, while exploring the ruins, have found a treasure trove of over 17,000 clay tablets inscribed with all sorts of messages. This library seems to be primarily governmental records. Almost every aspect of government, education, commerce, and business is covered. At first, 15,000 tablets were found in two rooms near the Royal Palace. (The Royal Library has not yet been found.)This number has now grown to over 17,000 with finds from other places in the excavation.

What has been found? So far more than 260 geographical locations have been mentioned. Such places as Sodom and Gomorrah are referred to in a bill of lading, shipping goods to those cities. Those insisting that there had never been a Sodom or Gomorrah have been proven wrong.

Lists of names of animals, fish, birds, professions, and many cities and people have been found. The list of animals, birds, and fish reminds us that in creation God had Adam name all the creatures. Vocabulary lists of over 1,000 words have been found with definitions of the words.

People's names are mentioned. People like Eber (Genesis 10:21), mentioned in the early chapters of Genesis and an ancestor of Abraham, are talked about. Many common names among the Israelites are often used, such as David, Saul, and Ishmael.

---

26 This Information is summarized from *The Archives of Ebla, An Empire Inscribed in Clay.*

BIBLICAL ARCHAEOLOGY

THE LANGUAGE OF EBLA

The language is Paleo-Canaanite, which is closely related to ancient Hebrew. The language could be referred to as Western Semitic.

One of the brightest professors the author has studied under was John Ralls. He made his life work studying the Semitic languages. He was proficient in all eleven of these languages. At the time of his death he was completing the lexicon for Acadian. This raises the question, what was the source of these languages? As descendants of Shem, they settled in what we think of as the Middle East, Canaan, Palestine, from the Nile northward to Haran. They divided into various tribes, like Abraham's sons Ishmael and Isaac did later, and became heads of nations. Ebla represents one of these language groups and streams.

Ancient languages are often hard to decipher. This was made easier because tablets, much like the Rosetta Stone, were found where three languages were side by side telling the same story. Eblaite was found next to a known language. Also it being related to Hebrew (a well-known Semitic language) has made it possible for it to be read and understood.

Names found in the tablets are common in the patriarchal accounts, indicating a relationship between the two historical streams. This has shown the biblical histories to be real, with clay tablets older than the biblical text, giving confirmation of what Moses wrote in the Pentateuch.

DATES OF THIS CIVILIZATION AND THE AREA IT RULED

Let us look more closely at the dates of this civilization. Ebla thrived 250 years before the patriarchs: Abraham, Isaac, Jacob, and Joseph. Ebla was there 1,000 years before the

Exodus from Egypt to Canaan. For some time Ebla had even ruled Egypt. Ebla apparently invaded and conquered Egypt for a time between the Egyptian Old Kingdom and the 12th dynasty of the Middle Kingdom. Just how long they ruled there is uncertain.

When Israel went to Egypt, foreign people (probably Hittites-Eblites) ruled. They may have been referred to as "Hyksos," and were possibly the kings who elevated Joseph to the position of second in command to pharaoh. The Hyksos were from Shem's line, as were the Hebrews and the people of Ebla. This could help explain how Joseph was able to rise to such a place of prominence in Egypt so quickly. This suggestion is not meant to discount the providence of God in Joseph's life.

Some old maps include the area where Ebla is under the Hittite Kingdom when they had ruled the whole area. The Hittites had ruled central Turkey and were still in existence when David was King in Israel. Bathsheba's husband was a Hittite. Uriah was a warrior in David's army. This helps explain why David had a Hittite in a key role in his army; they were from Shem's family tree, a common Semitic heritage.

RELATED TO THE HITTITE KINGDOM OF TURKEY

The Hittite Kingdom today is well remembered for what is called "The Valley of the 1,000 Hills." In central Turkey the Hittite kings and noblemen were buried in a common valley. At these funerals people brought a bucket of dirt and dumped it over the grave and this burial valley looks like giant moles had been active there. The more popular the leader was, the bigger the mound over his grave.

Ebla was no small village. Among the tablets was a census record that lists the population as 260,000. This would be no small town, but one of the major cities of the ancient world, possibly even for a short time the largest.

THE VALUE OF THE TABLETS

The value of all these tablets is that there are hundreds of confirmations of events, places, and people talked about in our Bible. Let us look at a list of some of these parallels.

Historians, when writing about their own history, may have been given to exaggeration. The records of these ancient kingdoms were sometimes extended backward, exaggerating when the kingdom started and the importance of what they accomplished. Politicians have not changed much.

Even though some accounts are exaggerated as to what has been found there, nevertheless, Ebla has been a wonderful boon to biblical studies. Here is what Ebla has done for our Bible: it has confirmed the high level of writing well before the Bible was written, well before Moses wrote the Pentateuch; there are hundreds of parallels between the Bible and the tablets; there are references to people, places and events talked about in our Bible.

Some of these tablets are two thousand years older than the Dead Sea Scrolls. They are valid written documents and records of their time.

Here are a few of the ways the Ebla tablets mention places found in the Bible and other similarities to our Bible:

   a) The Ebla tablets have proverbs and hymns, similar to those in the Bible.

   b) The cities of Kish, Ashdod, and Sidon are mentioned.

c) Words like "Adam-Melek," i.e., man-king is found, also showing that the name Adam was well known and used, as also the word for king.

d) "El" and "Ya" are used, similar to the Hebrew words for God, Elohim and Jehovah. Our words for God and Jehovah come from these two roots.

e) "Salim" is mentioned–the city of Melchizedek, or Jerusalem.

f) Hazor, Lachish, Megiddo, Gaza, Sinai, Ashdod, Joppa, Damascus, and "Urusalima" or Jerusalem are referred to; this is the oldest reference to Jerusalem ever found.

g) Sodom, Gomorrah, Admah, Zeboiim and Zoar, also called Bella, are mentioned.

h) Joppa and Damascus are spoken about. Damascus is the oldest continually inhabited city on earth.

i) Carchemish, (Isaiah 10:9) is mentioned.

j) A creation account very similar to Genesis 1—2 was found.

k) The Hittites are referred to well before Abraham bought the cave of Macpellah from a Hittite for a burial place for Sarah and later other members of his family. (The author has visited this cave more than once.)

l) Treaties and covenants that are very similar to those given by Moses have been found.

m) Laws of justice similar to those in the Pentateuch were found.

n) Ritualistic sacrifices, similar to those of Moses were found, but of a profoundly less spiritual nature.

So many subjects are discussed that help us know that the legal system was well advanced. Remember, this city came not long after the Tower of Babel.

o) If a man raped a virgin without her consent he was to be executed. This is very similar to what Moses said in Deuteronomy 22:22–30.

EBLA, EGYPT, AND CHINA'S BEGINNINGS

The oldest dynasties in China and Egypt began just after the flood of Noah and the Tower of Babel. Ebla came into existence about two hundred years after the flood. The Chinese histories say their founder was "Foa" or "Oah" who came from the great flood. The dates of China's founding coincide with those of Egypt, Ebla, and civilization in general that came from Mesopotamia. This brings credence to the Babel account.

NEO-ORTHODOX SCHOLARS PROVEN WRONG

The neo-orthodox German and French scholars insisted people did not know how to write that far back, or could only write at a very primitive level. The tablets prove that civilization was highly advanced. Building, mathematics, astronomy, and metallurgy were all well-advanced sciences. Could Noah have carried information about these subjects onto the ark with him?

EVOLUTIONISTS' THEORIES PROVEN UNTRUE

That man was just evolving from cavemen is a fiction taught by evolutionists and is not in line with the evidence. Even today, with our modern equipment, we would be hard pressed to build the Tower of Babel or the great pyramids.

The author has been in three of the largest pyramids where there are huge stones from Aswan, over three hundred miles away; they weigh hundreds of tons. The gigantic blocks are laid together so tightly that one cannot get a sharp knife blade between them in their 25–40 feet of length. Modern engineering would have a difficult time replicating this construction. These people were definitely brilliant.

Today we are separated from Bible events by thousands of years. God in his wisdom and love keeps giving us additional proof of the validity of His Word, the Bible. We have the Dead Sea Scrolls and now the 17,000-tablet Ebla library.

These do not make the Bible true; it always has been true. But they show that the Bible is a reliable historical record, not just a book telling us about God and His love for us.

Yes, these events happened a long time ago, but things like the Ebla Tablets make these events seem like they may have just happened.

The Bible stands every test of time and history. It is the Holy Word of God.

BIBLICAL ARCHAEOLOGY

Suggested Reading:
1.   Dr. Clifford Wilson, archaeologist, linguist, scholar, PhD. His book, *Ebla Tablets: Secrets of a Forgotten City*, Creation Life Publishers, San Diego, CA 1977.
2.   Dr. Giovanni Pettinato, archaeologist, linguist and translator. His book, *The Archives of Ebla: An Empire Inscribed in Clay*. Doubleday & Company, Inc., Garden City, New York, 1981.
3.   *Biblical Archaeology Review* magazine, various editions.
4.   And many others ...

Chapter Six

Ur of the Chaldees

Genesis 11:27–32 and 12:1–3 talk about Ur of the Chaldees. Just where is Ur of the Chaldees and the home from which Abraham and Sarah came? Ur is also spoken of in Nehemiah 9:7; it repeats that Abraham came from Ur of the Chaldees.

FINDING THE UR OF ABRAHAM AND SARAH

There are several ancient archaeological sites called Ur. It seems to be a common name used for more than one place. It is like our word Salem, or Decatur, with towns with the same name in more than one state.

Early archaeologists were confused and supposed that they had found Ur different places all the way from Haran to places both east and west in Mesopotamia. Today it is commonly believed that the biblical reference is to the Ur which is on the Euphrates River not far from the Persian Gulf. This is the site we will be examining. None of the objections to this location hold water.

The archaeologist Sir Leonard Woolley found a marble slab about five miles from Ur that said, "Annipadoa King of Ur son of Messanipadda." This tablet is in the British Museum in London, England. Woolley excavated Ur, and worked as an archaeologist from 1907 until 1949. He was recognized for his brilliance, hard work, and careful analysis of his findings. He was very well educated, with degrees from Oxford and, his excavation was done at a high level.

ARCHAEOLOGICAL EXCAVATION

Woolley had an excellent crew of more than 100 workers, and plenty of time to complete the task. He had the skills necessary to carefully evaluate what they found. He unearthed several impressive temples, thousands of graves, extensive residential areas, and many public buildings during the twelve seasons he excavated there.

Among his important finds were sixteen royal tombs, which were filled with many finely crafted items: precious stones, earrings, daggers, vessels, harps, beads, bracelets, a royal golden headdress, and a statue called, "I am caught in a thicket." This statue pictures a sheep caught in the brush. The Royal Headdress, made of gold, belonged to a queen named "Lady Duabi." They also found replicas of chariots and oxen among the royal tombs.

Another rather gruesome finding was a mass grave where it appears the people were drugged and buried alive with the monarch. This lack of concern for human life at Ur and with other pagan findings shows that Ur was a seriously wicked city. Abraham and Sarah were wise to leave there.

Another limestone slab, 5 x 14 feet, describes the building of the Ziggurat of Ur. This slab is in the Museum of Pennsylvania. There are other artifacts that mention this Ur. Ur was also referred to among the Ebla tablets.

As previously mentioned, ziggurats may have found their origin with the one previously being built at Babel, which was the first of its kind. The city from which they came had a ziggurat so they wanted one also. Not only have thirty of these been found around Mesopotamia, but the practice seems to have spread to Egypt, where not too much later the Step Pyramid was built, which closely resembles the ziggurats found in Mesopotamia. These massive structures are not only found in Mesopotamia and Egypt, but also they show up in Central and South America. What is the connection there?

It would be interesting to learn how people got from the Middle East to the Americas, bringing with them a building style that is a close match of those of earlier origin. This question will be considered in chapter 18.

Abraham's city was a center of literature and culture. This city dates more than 400 years before Moses and has shown the advanced level of civilization at that time. Writing was common, as were many of the modern conveniences we enjoy, like running water and flushing toilets. It is a figment of the imaginations of unbelieving teachers who subscribe to evolution and suppose ancient people were stupid, illiterate, and living in caves, when in reality as far back as evidence is available people were highly intelligent and accomplished remarkable things.

HAMMURABI'S CODE

In talking about Abraham, it is appropriate to mention Hammurabi's Code. Hammurabi, who was king of Babylon, was a contemporary of Abraham. Abraham was born about 2000 B.C., as was Hammurabi. The Tower of Babel came about 250 years before.

Genesis 14:1 says, "in the days of Amraphel (Hammurabi) king of Shinar …" Shinar was a term for Babylonia, including other cities in addition to Babylon. So Amraphel was king over Babylon and the extended area.

BIBLICAL ARCHAEOLOGY

The Code of Hammurabi, therefore, stands among a few of the most important archaeological document discoveries ever made. He had the scribes collect and codify the laws of his kingdom and had them engraved on stones to be set up in principal cities. One of these was set up in Babylon and one was found in the ruins of Susa, where it had been carried by an Elamite king who plundered Babylon. It is an eight-foot tall polished block of hard, black diorite stone, two feet wide and one-and-one-half feet thick. It has about 4,000 lines.

It discusses laws and rules Hammurabi said he received from the sun-god Shamash. These laws were the administration of justice, along with taxes, wages, interest, money-lending, property disputes, marriage, partnership, labor on public works, exemption from duty, canal building and care for the canals, regulations regarding passenger and freight service by canal and caravan, international commerce, and many other subjects.

Here is a book, written on stone, not a copy, about the size of an average Bible book, written in Abraham's day. It is still in existence in the Louvre Museum in Paris. The author has seen it on a couple of occasions. It is positive proof that literary skills and jurisprudence had reached a very high level in Abraham's day and long before Moses.

Some secularists have suggested that Moses just borrowed from Hammurabi's code for his Ten Commandments. Moses may or may not have known about Hammurabi's work, but nevertheless common sense and good laws would share common elements. The Law of Moses was much more extensive and covered the whole spectrum of life, human interaction and health. Much of what Moses wrote was more advanced than any other ancient law or system of living. His rules of health and purity are unequaled in any other civilization, suggesting their divine origin.

LIBRARIES WERE COMMON

In Abraham's day there were libraries in most cities: Lagash, Nippur, Sippar—in fact in every important city. There were thousands of books, schools, and temples; there were works on mathematics, astronomy, geography, religion and politics. Hammurabi was a great patron of learning.

When Abraham visited Egypt there were already thousands of inscriptions on stone, monuments, papyrus, and leather.

In the Ur of Abraham's day, Woolley uncovered tablets showing 150 school exercises, with mathematical, medical, and a complete conjugation of a Sumerian verb and its equivalent in Semitic, and much more. Ur was a modern city inhabited by brilliant people, who were idol worshippers and were very wicked.

ABRAHAM DISTRESSED BY UR'S SINFULNESS

Wickedness can come quickly. Most of us can recall more than one preacher's boy who turned his back on Christianity and gave way to his lower nature. In no time he began to deny the existence of God and involve himself in all sorts of carnal and disgusting sins. In the very next generation his children would have no idea of God. They would be open to worshipping all sorts of false gods, especially if this worship permitted them to live like alley cats.

Abraham was daily distressed by what he saw, and knew that there was only one true God, not hundreds. He knew that the lifestyle of the people was destructive. He was grieved. The knowledge of the one and only true God had been passed down from Noah to his children. It was well known in Ebla, where the names for God were often used. The people chose to live by lust and physical debauchery, rather than to follow the wholesome and holy will of God. It was much like today. Godly people are grieved by how wicked our culture has become, as was Abraham in his day.

Can you imagine how the conversation went when Abraham discussed with Sarah moving out of this modern city to live the rest of her life in tents? Remember that she must have been a beautiful woman, since on two occasions Abraham feared for his life, thinking someone would kill him to take her as their wife, even pharaoh of Egypt. He insisted she was his sister, which was a half-truth.

Abraham certainly had received from Shem the account of the creation and fall of man and of the Flood of Noah. He had a direct call from God to be the founder of a nation through which eventually all nations of the earth would be blessed. He came from a society that wrote and kept detailed records and histories of their nation. Abraham was a man of conviction and leadership. He must have kept accurate records of the accounts received from his ancestors. To these he added the accounts of his own life to pass on to his children.

Now let us turn our attention back to Ur, the city from which Abraham came. Ur is a "tel" city, with several layers built one upon the other. Ur had once been a seaport on the Persian Gulf and Euphrates River. It was one of the most beautiful and prosperous cities of its day. It was a center of agriculture, manufacturing, farming, and shipping. It had wonderfully fertile soil and wealth, with caravans and ships constantly coming and going. It shipped copper and hard stone to civilizations along the Persian Gulf.

The copious waters of the Euphrates and Tigris rivers that joined above their city, provided plenty of water to make the desert bloom with all sorts of crops, and the Persian Gulf provided cool moderating winds to make the area a pleasant place to live.

At about Abraham's time, Ur began to be more and more eclipsed by Babylon, which was up-river, but Ur remained an important city. By then the gulf had receded due to silting in of the harbor from flood waters from the Euphrates and Tigris Rivers that came from above. The waters of Ararat would come rushing down when the snows melted in the spring, bringing with it mud and silt that filled up the harbor, making Ur no longer a port city.

THE RUINS OF UR

There were several cities built one upon the other. Abraham's city was near the bottom, and consists of a tall mound, surrounded by lower subsidiary mounds, covering an area about two miles long northwest and southeast, and about a half-mile wide. Remnants of a surrounding wall, 70 feet thick and 80 feet high, have been traced for two-and-a-half miles. The temple area had an inner wall 1,200 feet by 600 feet. The University Museum of Pennsylvania and the British Museum, in a joint expedition, under the leadership of C. L. Woolley, worked four to five months each season for 12 years from 1922–1934 on this excavation. These ruins have been thoroughly explored.

The Ziggurat or Temple-Tower, with its idolatrous worship, was patterned after the Tower of Babel and is now the tallest mound, and in Abraham's day was the most conspicuous building in the city. It was last rebuilt by Nabonidus in the sixth century B.C. on the ruins of the one of Abraham's day.

The area where Abraham and Sarah lived has been identified and one can see a picture of it. As with others of these once

BIBLICAL ARCHAEOLOGY

prosperous cities, Ur today is just ruins covered by dust, sand, and dirt blown in from the surrounding desert.

The archaeologists have shown that our biblical record is a history of what actually took place, and even though these events happened nearly 4,000 years ago, they actually did occur.

TIMELINE CHART FROM THE FLOOD TO PYRAMIDS OF GIZA

Flood	Tower	Ebla	Abraham	Step	Giza
of Noah	of Babel	Syria	Ur	Pyramid	Pyramids
2348 B.C.	2248 B.C.	2240-30 B.C.	1996 B.C.	1950 B.C.	1750 B.C.

Please note:

1. Ancient Kingdoms sometimes exaggerated the age of their kingdoms.

2. From the flood to the Pyramids of Giza was 598 years.

3. Europe, China, the Middle East, and Africa cannot prove civilizations older than 2348 B.C., really before 2240 B.C. Older dates are exaggerations.

4. No pre-flood graveyards have been found.

5. The Step Pyramid, 1950 B.C.

   a) The earliest in Egypt
   b) Built by Pharoah Djoser
   c) It has six mastabas (levels) and is 203 feet high, 348 x 410 at the base.

d) The author has seen it many times. It was originally covered in white limestone, but today is in a state of decay.
  e) The associated burial complex covers many acres with a beautiful burial mortuary.

6. The Pyramids of Giza

    a) They are the largest and grandest pyramids
    b) The largest of them, Khufu=Cheops, was originally 481 feet high and remains the largest structure ever built by mankind.
    c) The second largest pyramid is Khafre=Chephren, originally 447 feet high.
    d) The third largest is Menkaura which is 228 feet high.
    e) Each of these was built as a burial chamber for a Pharaoh and his retinue.

Chapter Seven

Early Canaanite Cities or Tels

In our archaeological progression from Noah and the flood, to the Tower of Babel, Ebla, and Ur of the Chaldees, we now have brought our focus to the central lands of biblical history. We are now turning our attention to Palestine, or Canaan.

For many centuries mounds or hills around Palestine were noticed but not considered of any useful value. These hills had steep sides, but flat tops, thus were different looking from a normal hill that would have been cone shaped or round on top.

It was not until the archaeologists began to show interest that the importance of these flat-topped hills became evident. Today we will turn our attention to these hills, called "tels." Therefore, a tel is a steep sided hill, mound or heap. The Hebrew word "telula" means "steep," being a description of the steep sides of a tel. We will explain further about the shape as the discussion continues.

The Old Testament refers to these tels at least six times. This indicates that this city building plan practice was being used well before Israel invaded Canaan.

    Deuteronomy 13:16
    Joshua 8:28
    Jeremiah 49:12

DR. CHARLES CRANE

Ezekiel 3:15
Ezra 2:59
Nehemiah 7:61

One of James Michener's books, *The Source*, is a story built around a tel. He calls this tel "Macor" which is the Hebrew word for source. His story is built around a real tel, Megiddo. In this important novel he weaves a fictitious story around actual historical facts. The book gives a very good history of the inhabitants of Canaan from its first settlers until modern time.

Tels have their origin in the historical period when Canaan did not have a centralized government, but many small city states, similar to our counties in the United States. Actually, hundreds of these small villages existed throughout Israel and Mesopotamia.

Here is a short list of some tels that have been examined by archaeologists.

Tel Aviv	Tel Megiddo	Tel Shimron
Tel Yokneam	Tel Kassis	Tel Agol
Tel Dor	Tel Regeu	Tel Par
Tel Kisson	Tel Bira	Tel Akko
Tel Shiloh	Tel Afek	Tel Sarid
Tel Hazor	Tel Dan	Tel Lachish
Tel Gamma	Tel Issachar	Tel Ashkelon

The author has seen and walked around many of these ancient tel cities. Many more could be named. When one becomes familiar with this ancient city construction concept, many can be observed by just driving around Israel. A lot of archaeological excavation remains to be done.

BIBLICAL ARCHAEOLOGY

THE FOUNDING OF A TEL

In choosing a site to build their village, two things were sought: a hill and a good fresh water source nearby. For example, the name Tel Aviv means Tel (a steep hill), Aviv (the Hebrew word for water spring). Thus, they looked for a place easily fortified near a source of fresh water, a tel-aviv.

Once they had chosen the site, a wall was built around the perimeter of the hill, making it easier to defend against thieves, raiders or armies. The tel was a citadel to which those farming the area or living outside the tel's walls could retreat at night or during raids.

Not all tels are visible today. Present Jerusalem is 30–50 feet above the Jerusalem of King David and even the city of Jesus' day. It was built on a hill, with a wonderful fresh water supply nearby, the Gihon Spring.

TELS' NATURAL TENDENCY TO GROW

There were natural reasons why tels grew higher over time. Palestine is on the Rift Valley that runs all the way from Africa into Europe. Earthquakes were and are common along this fault line. These villages would often be shaken down. It was easiest to rebuild with materials already there. After destruction by earthquake, war, or just deterioration over time the tel was leveled off and useable material was requisitioned to build again.

Another reason for their growth was garbage. One archaeologist said, "It appears half of the ancient world was making pottery and the other half breaking it." They did not have garbage service like we do, so they threw out the broken pottery. Dirt from cleaning and dust storms and torrential rains all conspired to destroy their mud-dried-brick houses and to cause the sites to need rebuilding repeatedly. As many as 27 cities built one on top of another have been found.

Wars would destroy the walls and housing. After the battle it was easiest to rebuild as a lot of the material needed was already there.

Each rebuild made the city more easily defended as the hill grew higher.

Sites were built over and over again. Under the ruins were lots of building materials. The water works were still there. A new site and city would require a new infrastructure; at the old site these things were still there. The old city was built on a prime location. The walls had been made of things that would last and the materials were still there and did not have to be gathered. Houses were made of sun-dried brick and mud was easily found to make more. Each new destruction and rebuild made the city easier to defend as the slope to the walls was higher and steeper. Finally, surviving people still owned their building plot where they could rebuild.

THE DEATH OF TELS

As the country grew, the small tel sites became too small to accommodate the additional population. They needed bigger and better locations. With the coming of a centralized government, the government took up the responsibility for the common defense. Or they found a larger or more convenient or easier place to build and strongly fortify as their enemies grew stronger.

Tel sites, after being deserted, became places for watch towers, or bunkers in times of war. They continued to be used, but not as villages. In time dust, dirt, and decay left them as funny looking flat-topped hills.

BIBLICAL ARCHAEOLOGY

THE VALUE OF TELS TODAY

The tels of modern Israel have become treasure troves for archaeological excavation. Places like Tel Dan, Tel Aviv, and Tel Beit Shean have grudgingly given up their secrets and we have learned so much that augments our biblical studies. They have become a physical history book about earlier events, people, and customs. They often yield up evidence for people, places, and events in our Bibles.

Much has been learned about natural disasters, human diseases, and human caused disasters. Nations and people have been identified. Famous people's existence has been verified.

LET'S EXAMINE THREE WELL-KNOWN TELS

1. Laish or Tel Dan, Genesis 14:1–16, especially V:14
   Things found at Tel Dan. A stone inscribed with the words "David, King of Israel." Here is the only ancient gate to one of these tel sites that is totally intact. It is the gate Abraham might have entered when he and his troops went to rescue Lot and the other Kings of the Plain. Joshua could have entered here many years later.

2. Tel Beit Shean, I Samuel 31:1-13
   The Temple of Ashtaroth has been found where Saul and his sons' bodies and armor were taken, as well as the walls of the city where their bodies were hung. The city is near Mt. Gilboah where Saul and Jonathan were killed by the Philistines.
   Beit Shean, or Bethshan, was one of the ten cities of the Decapolis, the only one on the west side of the Jordan River.

3. Tel Aviv is not mentioned in our Bible, but is the capital of Israel today. The ancient tel remains near the new city. It does not appear to have yet been excavated.[27]

Suggested Reading:
An internet search for these sites will give you more information and pictures to illustrate what has been written here.

---

27 The author has visited these tels.

Chapter Eight

Sodom, Gomorrah, and Petra

Death at the Dead Sea

WHERE DID MOAB, AMMON, AND EDOM COME FROM?

The scripture text that talks about Sodom is found in Genesis 18:16—19:29. Why is this chapter important to our study? Abraham's nephew Lot moved to Sodom and Gomorrah and was caused to leave there because the city was so sinful. After Lot left Sodom, his daughters got him drunk and he impregnated both of them, producing two sons, Moab and Ben-Ammi, or Ammon. These fathered the two nations of Moab and Ammon.

The third nation that was constantly a thorn in Israel's side was Edom. Edom was the son of Esau and fathered the Edomites, who became a nation and settled in Petra. Each of these nations had their origin in troubled families. Lot and his daughters came from Sodom.

LOOKING FOR SODOM AND GOMORRAH

Jesus refers to the day of His second coming as being like Sodom (Luke 17:26-32). As was true with the destruction of the flood of Noah and the destruction of Sodom and Gomorrah, both were times of unspeakable wickedness, much like many places in our nation today. There was lying, greed, brutality, beastliness, beheadings, sexual depravity, and criminal activities seldom seen in history. It was a center of homosexual depravity.

Our task in locating Sodom and Gomorrah is made more difficult for several reasons. First, the biblical text says they were burned up and their smoke went up to heaven like a great furnace.

Another problem for the archaeologists has been the changing levels of the Dead Sea. The water level is thought to have been lower in the days of Abraham. When archaeologists began their search for Sodom and Gomorrah, the ruins were most likely under water.

The area must have been much more verdant than it is today. Today it is a barren wasteland. The reason for the change is uncertain, but may relate to the area west having had much more vegetation, trees and crop land than there is today, especially toward the coast. Because of the vegetation on the plains to the west, they would have had increased moisture and this would naturally cause more rainfall inland.

The Dead Sea is 1,000 feet deep at the northern end, but only 10–20 feet deep when the search began for the cities of Sodom and Gomorrah. Anyone who has gone swimming in the Dead Sea knows how caustic it is, with its 37-percent mineral content. For early archaeologists, there was no way to examine under the sea. Even today it is a disgusting liquid that makes it difficult to explore under water. It is caustic to equipment and painful to eyes. It is not a place to boat or waterski.

Over the past forty years of visiting the sea, the author has observed that each year the water level has receded. The reason for this is that Israel and Jordan use the water of the

BIBLICAL ARCHAEOLOGY

Jordan River and its tributaries for irrigation, the Dead Sea is drying up, and about a third of its southern end is now dry land. This has made exploration now possible.

When archaeologists tried to find the location of Sodom, for a long time they looked for clues unsuccessfully. One clue they finally found was the mountains at the southwestern end of the sea which are called "Usdom." Could this mean "Sodom"? They believed it did.

In the area, they had already found the biblical city of Zoar, one of the five cities of the plains of Genesis 14. They had also found a massive graveyard in the vicinity, indicating that at one time there was a large population there. Tens of thousands of graves were found. Some of these graves are unique. They sank a shaft into the ground and buried people in tubes off of this shaft all around, deeper and deeper. Whole families could be, and were, buried in one shaft.

Also, this is the area where Lot's wife was turned to a pillar of salt. She was warned to not look back at the destruction of the city. She did, with disastrous results. There are several large salt pillars near this area; one is referred to as Lot's wife. Without a doubt, after all these years, it is not the same pillar she became, but it does show that the people of the area still believe this is where Sodom and Gomorrah were.

These cities are referred to in the Ebla tablets, which helps prove that the cities did exist. That there is so little left of them confirms the Bible account that says they were burned up. Today Sodom and Gomorrah's locations have been positively identified.

Two men were talking about Lot's wife becoming a pillar of salt because she looked back to Sodom. One said he could not believe such a story to which the other replied, "I have no trouble believing this at all, as my wife looked back and turned into a telephone pole."

HOW WERE THEY DESTROYED?

How were they destroyed? Of course God need not use natural means, but could employ any method He wished. Everything from a meteorite to an earthquake has been suggested as the cause of the destruction. There could be a natural explanation. Genesis 14:10 and 19:24 says there were "slime pits" nearby, which would indicate petroleum. This area still has layers of petroleum, sulfur and salt. This, if ignited, could cause a mighty conflagration. Have you seen sulfur set on fire? It burns like a Roman candle. The text says there was sulfur.

Excavation of the area has found sulfur balls—an indication of destruction by fire of the area where the cities were thought to have been.

Lot and his daughters escaped, and Lot's incestuous sons Moab and Ammon became the fathers of two tribes that became mortal enemies of Israel. Jacob's (Israel) brother Esau's son Edom became the father of the other tribe—the Edomites—who also were enemies of Israel. We will now turn our attention to Edom and their capital, Petra.

PETRA AND THE DESCENDANTS OF LOT AND ESAU

After Lot and his two daughters fled from Sodom, they came to Zoar but resided in the hill country nearby, for Lot was afraid to live in the city. One can understand his feelings (Genesis 19:30–38). It must have been a lonely existence for the young women, his daughters.

Lot's daughters conspired to get their father drunk so that he might impregnate them both. The result was that two sons were born of incest to them. The first was named Moab and the second was named "Ben-ammi." One became the father of the Moabites and the second the Ammonites. They became the perpetual enemies of Israel. Today the cities of Amman and Petra, Jordan, remain as reminders of this past history.

The third group was descended from Esau, Jacob's brother who was disinherited because he sold his birthright for a bowl of red stew. His younger brother Jacob received his blessing and Jacob's name was changed to Israel after he wrestled with the angel all night at the Jabbok River.

The three small nations across the Jordan from Israel were Moab, most northerly, then Ammon, (now Jordan with its capital called Amman) and then Edom, most southern. It is here that we find Petra or Sela, in the mountains of Seir.

SEIR, PETRA, AND SELA

The mountains of Seir run all the way from the Gulf of Aqaba to the southern end of the Dead Sea. It is in these mountains that Petra is found. The word Edom is akin to the Hebrew word red, which describes the color of Petra. Edom was the name given to Esau's son, as he may also have been of red-haired complexion.

Sela is a more proper name for the rock-hewn city that is now called Petra. The Greek word Petra has stuck, because it is a city hewn out of the solid rock. Petra is the Greek word for rock.

The Edomites were rascals. They refused Israel entrance into Palestine when they came to Palestine in the exodus from Egypt (Numbers 20:14–21). They were their relatives, but they treated Israel like mortal enemies.

When Israel actually entered Palestine, the Edomites remained their enemies. They are referred to repeatedly in the prophetical books because of their evil deeds towards Israel and the surrounding nations.

Petra was a city that was very easily defended. The eastern entrance to the city was through a narrow gorge, called the Siq, with high perpendicular walls on each side. This entrance was about a quarter of a mile long. On the western side of the city were cliffs that drop off into the Rift Valley south of the Dead Sea. Part of this western side of the city was defended by a high wall. This meant that the city could be easily defended by just a few well-armed soldiers. The Siq was primarily and essentially the only entrance to the city.

Through this narrow entrance ran a clear stream of water to supply all their water needs. It was piped and also run through a channel in the solid rock wall that led into town. In times of flood a diversion channel was made that routed water around the city and over the cliff.

The Edomites would wait until harvest was over in Israel and other surrounding communities, and then come out armed to the teeth and by force steal what the others had grown. Then they would retire to their mountain fortress to enjoy the fruits of their spoils. They brought bloodshed and havoc to their neighbors and relatives. They were in reality—bandits.

David's General Joab conquered them, killing 12,000 of them and they were subjugated until they gained their independence during Judah's decline. They again became a source of harm and destruction to Israel (II Samuel 8:14).

The sixtieth Psalm is written about Joab's victory over surrounding nations and Edom in particular. David said, "Upon Edom I have cast my shoe." This shows his disdain for them.

BIBLICAL ARCHAEOLOGY

This reminds us of the Arab that threw a shoe at President George W. Bush, but hit his press secretary instead.

There are many prophecies against Edom in the Minor Prophets for their violent and evil ways. These prophecies have been fulfilled today and Petra is just ruins. There were many other inhabitants of Petra over the years, and many who conquered Petra, including the Romans. Various architectural styles are found, indicating which conqueror did the work.

J. L. Burckhardt was the rediscoverer of Petra. He had visited the ruins of Palmyra and Baalbeck and the great trading city of Damascus. He suffered a lot trying to find the ancient fabled places. He was deserted by his guides and servants, leaving him alone in the desert to die. But he was made of hardy stuff and was not easy to kill or dissuade. Finally on August 22, 1812, he saw the ruins of Wadi Mousa and believed them to be those of ancient Petra. He was right.

Burckhardt was a well-educated man, with huge stamina, and was not easily deterred. He passed through many dangers and found Petra because of his strength of character, his natural courage in adversity, and ability to survive in all sorts of crises.

Still today the excavation at Petra is still in its beginning stages. No one has found any evidence dating back to the fourth century B.C. So far excavation has only reached to the second and first century B.C. Only about 15% of what is there has been explored. 85% is still unexplored, underground and untouched.

CONCLUDING THOUGHTS

We have made our way from Noah and his family as they left the Ark, to the Tower of Babel, Ebla, China, Egypt, and to

Petra. All along the way we have found archaeological information that demonstrates the Bible's historical and geographical accuracy.

We have found the home town of the Patriarch Abraham and his beautiful wife Sarah. We have followed their journeys to Haran, Palestine, Egypt, and back to the homeland that God had promised Abraham.

We have looked at Lot and his misadventures in the cities of Sodom and Gomorrah. He was captured by the four kings of Shinar, Ellasar, Elam, and Goiim, and Abraham had to rescue him. We have journeyed to Tel Dan and several of the other ancient cities of Palestine where Abraham, the patriarchs, and Joshua would have visited.

We have looked at the destruction of Sodom and Gomorrah and how Lot became the father of two nations—Moab and Ammon—through his incestuous relationship with his two daughters. We have learned that Moab and Ammon became a thorn in the side of Abraham's seed, the chosen seed from which the Messiah was to come.

We have shown how Esau became the father of a rather worthless lot, the Edomites. They settled in Mt. Seir and in the city of Sela, or Petra. These became constant enemies of Israel and from their fortress city raided and plundered their neighbors. We will next turn our attention to Egypt, the Land of Goshen, and the Pyramids.

Suggested Reading:
Genesis 18:22—19:38.

Chapter Nine

Egypt, the Pyramids, and Goshen

As we continue our journey, we will now visit Egypt. Egypt is important archaeologically because it was a place visited by Father Abraham, where Israel lived for over 400 years, and was the place our Lord Jesus spent part of His youth. Still today Egypt is a most fascinating place.

Egypt had been founded by Ham's son. We read in Genesis 10:6, "The sons of Ham: Cush, Egypt, Put, and Canaan" (ESV). In some Bible versions Egypt is called "Mizraim." They are one and the same person and he is sometimes called "Menes."

Egypt, Mesopotamia, and Africa were where Ham's descendants settled. Another grandson of Ham was named Nimrod. He was a mighty hunter and founded Babel (Babylon) and other cities. He went to Assyria and founded Nineveh.

Recall that Shem became the father of the Semitic races, from which the Hebrews and Israel descended. Japheth became the father of the European nations. Noah fathered the Chinese and Far Eastern nations.

We know for sure that Egypt was begun by Ham's son Egypt. This makes the country of Egypt quite interesting in archaeological studies. This also helps us know that the influence of Babel would have certainly been felt there. This is shown architecturally in the earliest pyramids.

It is not surprising to find the influence of ziggurat building in the early and later pyramids of Egypt. Egypt plays a consistent place in the history of Abraham, his seed, and Israel until the time of Christ and beyond.

In the third century B.C. it was in Egypt that the Septuagint, (from Hebrew to Greek) translation of the Old Testament was made and was where the Coptic Church began through the ministry of Mark, the writer of the second Gospel. Egypt still plays an important part in our world today. It deserves a place in our study of biblical archaeology.

EGYPTIAN PYRAMIDS

The Sphinx and Pyramids of Giza are the grandest of the pyramid era and have garnered the most attention of people for most of modern history. But each year the number of pyramids grows as more are unearthed from the sand. On one of the author's earlier trips to Egypt he was told there were 72 pyramids. More recently the number has grown to 138. It is likely that this number will continue to grow.

The Giza pyramids are the only remaining of the seven ancient wonders of the world. As one historian says, "They were built at the very dawn of history." Sir Flinders Petrie said, "They are the greatest and most accurate structures the world has ever seen." Britannica says, "The brain power to which they testify is as great as that of any modern man." The Giza pyramids are perfectly aligned with the four directions, North, South, East and West.

Dating of the pyramids of Egypt varies. It appears there is a tendency to want to make them older than they really are. The various dates should not detract from their reality. You may wish to differ with the dates assigned them in this book, which is entirely your privilege.

BIBLICAL ARCHAEOLOGY

Here is a list of some of them, from earliest to latest. (These dates are somewhat arbitrary and could be extended backward 200–300 years. If this is done then the Flood and Babel would also be that much earlier.)

Pyramid/Pharaoh	Reign	Field
Djozer (step)	2200–1950 BC	Saqqara
Sneferu (bent)		Dashur
Sneferu (red)		Dashur
Sneferu (ruined)		
Meidum		
Khufu		Giza
Djedefre		
Abu Rawash		
Khafre		Giza
Menkaure		
Giza		
Sahure		Abusir
Neferirkare Kakai		Abusir
Nyuserre Ini		Abusir
Amenemhat I		Lisht
Senusret I		
Lisht		
Senusret II		
el-Lahun		
Amenemhat III	1850–1750 BC	Hawara

The exact purpose of the pyramids is uncertain. The Tower of Babel was built as a tower to reach God, possibly the moon god. At least the effort was not to deify mankind but to point to some sort of belief in a supreme being. They should have known better since they descended from a heritage that believed in the one and only true God.

The ziggurats that followed the Tower of Babel were built with an idolatrous temple on top in which all sorts of sinful things took place. The pyramids appear to have been built to assure the immortality of the Pharaoh. This was likely because he was seen as a man-god, or deity. The pyramids may have been seen as a sort of resurrection machine in which everything the Pharaoh would need in the future life was included. For sure they were a funeral place for a deified man or woman.

The Djedefre, son of Khufu, pyramid has become a place of stone quarrying, as was the Tower of Babel. To a lesser extent this is true of other pyramids. The white limestone coverings of the Pyramids of Giza have been taken to build things in Cairo, leaving only a small cap on the largest one.

The English Standard Version translates Genesis 10:6, "Cush, Egypt, Put, and Canaan." The American Standard Version says, "Cush, Mizraim, Put, and Canaan." Why is this difference important? It is important because the earliest Pharaoh in Egyptian history records was "Menes" or Mizraim. The ESV says Egypt, and Egypt founded Egypt, and he was called Menes.

The Step Pyramid was the first pyramid. It began as a large mastaba, a square flat-topped mound. Four more mastabas, each smaller than the one below, were added on top of each other. When finished, this pyramid was 204 feet high.

The engineers looked for a place where there was solid rock for a foundation for the pyramids. To level the rock for building, a trench was made around the perimeter that was filled with water. When the water was uniformly deep all the way around, they knew they had the base level. When they had the base level, they laid a limestone or granite layer over the base upon which to build.

BIBLICAL ARCHAEOLOGY

Earlier pyramids were made of smaller stones. These stones were quarried nearby. The Pyramids of Giza were built of massive stones. The largest was built by Snefru's son, Khufu, known also as Cheops, the later Greek form of his name.

Cheops' base covers 13 acres and its sides rise at a 51 degrees 52 minutes angle and were over 755 feet long. It originally stood 481 feet high. Today it is 450 feet high. Its stones are estimated to weigh from two tons to the largest weighing more than fifteen tons, or 30,000 pounds. There are 2,300,000 of these stones. It boggles the mind to think of how much labor went into building these pyramids.

It has been suggested that slaves were made to do the work. Today this idea has been replaced with the belief that the work was done by farmers or village workers who were not busy while their crops grew. It is thought that the Cheops pyramid took 100,000 men twenty years to build.

Inside the pyramids were burial chambers made of rose granite. The limestone for the majority of the blocks came from a nearby quarry. Some limestone came from Tura, across the Nile, and the large rose-granite stones inside came from Aswan, 300 miles up the Nile River. This rose granite has been found as far away as Baalbeck, seventy miles inland in what is Syria today. It would have been brought from Aswan down the Nile, across the Mediterranean Sea and then to Baalbeck. The task seems impossible.

Pyramids did not stand alone, but were part of a group of buildings which included temples, chapels, other tombs, and mortuaries. The Pharaoh's body was probably mummified in the mortuary building while the temples were used for funeral services. After embalming, it was taken by underground tunnel to its final resting place.

There has been plenty of speculation about pyramid construction. Egyptians had copper tools (Possibly iron tools also) such as chisels, drills, and saws that may have been used to cut the relatively soft stone. The hard granite used for burial chamber walls and some of the exterior casing, would have posed a more difficult problem. Workmen may have used an abrasive powder, such as sand, with the drills and saws. Knowledge of astronomy was necessary to orient the pyramids to the cardinal points, and water-filled trenches probably were used to level the perimeter. A tomb painting of a colossal statue being moved shows how huge stone blocks were moved on sledges over ground first made slippery by liquid. The blocks were then brought up ramps to their positions in the pyramid. Finally, the outer layer of casing stones was finished from the top down and the ramps dismantled as the work was completed.

The massive granite pieces from Aswan had to be ferried on barges down river and then moved up to the site. This was an incredible engineering task.

The stones were moved up inclined slopes to their final resting places. The builders had to be brilliant to devise the plan to move the stones without the aid of modern machinery, which even today would present a formidable task.

THE STEP PYRAMID

Now let us talk briefly about a few of the more notable pyramids. First, notice the Step Pyramid of Djoser. This is thought to have been built during the Third Dynasty. The builder was Imhotep, one of the earliest known architects and engineers. This was the first monumental stone building constructed in Egypt. The idea probably came from the Tower of Babel and ziggurats of Mesopotamia.

The next several pyramids were built in a similar style. Snefru's reign marks the change from step to cased or true pyramid. His four completed projects set the stage for his successors, who built the famous complex at Giza. Some pyramids were made of mud or fired brick around a rubble core; they were economy models.

THE BENT PYRAMID

Snefru's first pyramid at Dahshur was called the Bent Pyramid. It was the first true pyramid. At first, its walls had a 60 degree angle. When the pyramid reached the height of 131 feet, cracks developed in the interior corridors and the outer casing, probably due to the steep angle of the walls and the gigantic weight of the stone blocks.

Engineers placed a girdle around the lower levels and built the upper part of the pyramid at a 43 degree angle. Archaeologists found two burial chambers, although there could still be undiscovered chambers or passageways inside this pyramid.

THE RED PYRAMID

Snefru also built the Red Pyramid at Dahshur, with a red limestone core. The interior structure was much less complex than that of the Bent Pyramid.

THE LAND OF GOSHEN

In Genesis 45:9–10, Joseph, second ruler in Egypt, sent for his family and promised that they would live in the land of Goshen (in our language). (The Hebrew name was Arets Gosen.) We are not sure what the word Goshen means, maybe cultivated, or inundated. Both would be true. It is the land near the Nile delta that was well suited for agriculture and herdsmen.

Since Israel was having a serious famine that was predicted to last five more years, the sons of Israel made the trek to Egypt and settled in Goshen. Goshen has been said to be the best land in all of Egypt.

It is thought that this land was somewhat separated from the more populated parts of Egypt. Egyptians worshiped animals and created things. This may seem strange, but today we have people that value creatures more than humans. In America today one can buy animal medical insurance, there are animal graveyards, animal go-to-work days and now animal work week breaks. At the same time human babies are expendable. Genesis 46:34 says that shepherds were an abomination to the Egyptians.

So Israel came to dwell in Egypt for 430 years (Galatians 3:17 and Exodus 12:40–41). In the beginning this was a good arrangement, but as time passed Israel was more and more enslaved. They were forced to build store cities and their work load was increased more and more and became just plain slavery. Two of the cities in Goshen were Ramses and Pithom.

Two store cities have been excavated and the archaeologists found that the early mud brick had lots of straw, but as Pharaoh made the bondage much more severe and did not provide straw to put in the sun-dried mud bricks, the brick had less and less straw as the buildings grew towards completion. This is a confirmation of what the Bible says about Pharaoh demanding more and more from the Israelite slaves.

A Pharaoh that did not know Joseph came to power. It is commonly believed that the period when the Hyksos invader kings ruled that they were sympathetic to Israel. When the Egyptians regained their independence, they were not sympathetic to Israel.

BIBLICAL ARCHAEOLOGY

We have already said that the Hyksos Kings were probably Hittites and these rulers were either from Ebla or Turkey (Exodus 1:8). It is possible that these were the foreign rulers who for a time ruled in Egypt. This made it possible for Joseph to so quickly rise to power in Egypt.

When the Egyptians overthrew these foreigners and again ruled their land, the Israelites became a threat to them. With this new Pharaoh in power they feared that Israel might side with their enemies or Israel themselves try to conquer Egypt, so they began to kill the baby boys and enforce cruel slavery. Pharaoh declared that all the baby boys were to be thrown into the Nile to drown. When Moses was born, his mother put him in a tar-covered basket and set him afloat in the Nile, where Pharaoh's daughter found him and adopted him. Moses grew up with all the education and benefits of being Pharaoh's grandson, qualifying him to lead Israel out of bondage.

In regard to our study of archaeology, Egypt is important because of Abraham, Israel, and Jesus having lived there. Many of the wonders we see today, Abraham, Israel, and Jesus also saw.

For many years it was thought that there was no historical mention, outside the Bible, of Israel having been in Egypt. This is no longer true. At Memphis, in the land of Goshen, is a large stone monument that tells about Israel's time spent in Egypt. The author has seen this stone, which is about 6 x 1.5 x 3.5 feet. Aza, his friend Safwat Sadek's daughter, fluent in cuneiform and hieroglyphics, has read it to him. It confirms the biblical record of Israel's time in Goshen.

In the Cairo museum there is another large stone, about 12 feet tall, that also has the inscribed story of Moses and the Children of Israel being in Egypt. It says that Merenptah was the Pharaoh of Moses' time. He was the thirteenth son of Ramses II and of the nineteenth dynasty, about 1250 B.C. (However this could have been as much as 200 years earlier.)

Suggested Reading:
Genesis 12:10–20. Abraham and Sarah in Egypt.
       46–47. Children of Israel in Egypt
Matthew 2:13–15. Jesus in Egypt
There is a lot of interesting information about Egypt on the internet.

Chapter Ten

Jericho

The Red Sea Crossing

Exodus 14:15-29 tells about the Red Sea crossing and the children of Israel's exodus from Egypt. There is ample evidence to believe this crossing is an actual historical event. Today the event is not in question, but the place of the event is. New evidence has come to light but how factual this information is, is still under question.

UNCERTAIN WHERE ISRAEL CROSSED

There are two different crossing site points of view, with both making a strong case for their opinions. It may be that the Red Sea, Gulf of Aqaba site is more probable. It is near the land of Midian, where Moses was a shepherd for forty years. It is here that claimed finds seem to prove it as the place of crossing. This is on the Gulf of Aqaba rather than the Gulf of Suez, and is one of the two gulfs that run northward out of the Red Sea. Both locations can be considered to be the Red Sea.

If this is the right location, there is only one place where the crossing could have been probable, as the Gulf of Aqaba is a mile deep all along except in one place where it is only 2,500 feet deep. A pillar was reported to have been found on the shore at this location, but it was so weathered it could not be read. Archaeologists searched on the other side of the Gulf, and another pillar similar to the other was said to have been found under the water, encrusted with coral. This one could be read and it said it was placed there by King Solomon and marked the place where Israel crossed the sea. When divers explored under water, they found chariot wheels encased in coral and human bones among the coral. One set of gold-covered chariot wheels was found. Those who claimed these finds have sometimes been over zealous and their reliability has been questioned by some. Time will either validate or disprove these claims.

The debate is heated at this time, and the issue is not settled. It does seem incredible that physical evidence such as bones and chariot wheels could be found of something that happened so long ago. Space does not permit a full discussion of this location as the place of the crossing at this point.

Across the sea in the land of Midian, there is a mountain that could have been the Mount where Moses received the Ten Commandments. According to those who insist this is the correct Mount of Moses, they point to several features of this mountain that match the biblical narrative.

The other site for the Red Sea crossing would have been just east of the Land of Goshen and across what is now the Suez Canal. This would take them to the long-believed Mount of Moses location at the Monastery of St. Catherine, centrally located in the Sinai Peninsula. It has long been thought that this is not the correct place of the Mt of Moses. More work is needed to sort out the correct place where Moses received the words from God and Israel crossed the Red Sea.[28]

---

28   Blum, Howard; *The Gold of Exodus, Discovering the True Site of Mt. Sinai.*

BIBLICAL ARCHAEOLOGY

JERICHO

After forty years of wandering in the wilderness, Israel came to enter the land promised to their father Abraham. Their entry point was just across the river from the small fortified city of Jericho.

So let us turn our attention to Jericho. After the death of Moses, one of the two spies that gave a positive report of Canaan was Joshua, who was chosen to lead Israel.

Israel was camped across the Jordan River from Jericho in Ammon, not far from the present day city of Amman, Jordan. They camped just above the Dead Sea. It was spring time and the melting snow of Mount Hermon caused the Jordan River to be at flood stage, overflowing all its banks and making it impossible for people to cross.

God caused the waters to be stopped upriver at a place called Adam (or a dam was made at Adam). Israel was able to cross without wading water and a stone was picked up by one of each of the tribes to make a monument of their crossing on the western side of the river in the land of Canaan.

Now Israel was in enemy territory with a flooding river behind them and God instructed Joshua to circumcise all the men. This rite had been neglected during their forty years in the wilderness. It must have tested their faith to incapacitate all the warriors of Israel for many days after arriving and being camped in enemy territory. Joshua 2:1–22; 3:5 and chapter 6 tell of these events. Especially important is 6:20.

HISTORY AND AGE OF JERICHO

Jericho was a tel, and like most tels was built next to a wonderful flowing spring of water, today referred to as the Spring of Elijah, who later purified the water which before had tasted bad (II Kings 2:19–22). This spring today still has a large volume of water, enough to supply the needs of a significant city and irrigate the nearby fields.

Some early archaeologists claimed that Jericho is the oldest city ever found on earth, possibly 7,000–9,000 years old. They were partly right and partly wrong. It does appear to be one of the earliest cities found after the flood.

This would have been a choice site for a village since it was a semi-tropical paradise, with plentiful water, warm climate, and the ability to grow things year around; it could be thought of as an ancient Yuma, Arizona. No pre-flood cities have been found, so Bible believers do not accept that it is as old as some today claim. Jericho has to be dated later but still could be among the earliest cities after the flood, being founded by those who came from Noah's lineage and who came from Babel. We can be fairly certain that this city was founded either by Ham's son Canaan, or possibly one of the children of Shem.

Another very ancient city is Damascus, which is located not too many miles north of Jericho. It also has a great climate and fine water supply furnished by two rivers that flow from Mount Hermon. It also is a city with a most pleasant climate, with the desert to the east and the mountains to the west. It is thought to be the oldest city on earth which has been continually inhabited. Certainly this is true of the Middle East.

Jericho not only had water from the spring of Elijah but also had access to the plentiful waters of the Jordan River which would also have been a good source of fish for food. Today there are still many fishing fleets on Galilee and these fish would have migrated downstream. Still today there are deer and gazelles in this area.

BIBLICAL ARCHAEOLOGY

ARCHAEOLOGICAL EXCAVATIONS

Charles Warren (1868) was the first to excavate and claimed that he found nothing of real value at Jericho. Unfortunately he had excavated just a few feet away from what would have been a very rewarding find. He just quit too soon.

The earliest archaeologist to make a more careful examination of Jericho was Carl Watzinger, who excavated in 1907 and 1909–1911. He found collapsed mud brick walls and dated this find to about the 14th century B.C. which would coincide with the time of Joshua and the conquest of Canaan. He was disappointed in not finding much that he had hoped for. Later excavations showed he also had quit too soon and chosen an unfortunate place to excavate.

Dr. John Garstang excavated from 1929–1936. He found pottery that helped with dating (even today pottery is considered a great help in dating), and evidence of the city's destruction about 1400 B.C. He is a second witness to the city's destruction in the time of Joshua. He found stone jars still filled with grain, and other evidence that the city had been burned and not looted. Food supplies would have been of great value to people coming in from the desert. The food was left because it was devoted to God as the first fruits of Israel's new home.

Kathleen Kenyon excavated from 1952–1958 and probably did the best archaeological job and made the most significant finds, including the pre-Joshua city tower that remains the most remarkable structure that has yet been found.

Lorenzo Nigro and Nkola Marcelti excavated from 1997–2000.

Here is the gist of what these excavations have concluded about ancient Jericho:

DR. CHARLES CRANE

1. There were two walls around the city of Joshua's time. These walls were about 15 feet apart. The outer wall was about 6 feet thick and the inner wall was 12 feet thick. These walls were about 30 feet high. These double walls are called casemite walls.

2. Houses were built between the walls to strengthen and stabilize the walls.

3. The walls had faulty, uneven foundations and were not carefully built.

4. When Jericho was destroyed by Joshua, the outer wall fell outward and the inner wall was pulled down by the houses that connected them. This caused them to tumble down the steep incline upon which the tel was built.

5. The archaeologists felt the walls had been shaken down by a strong earthquake. This conclusion was supported by large cracks in the floors of the houses. To this day this whole area is still an earthquake prone zone. It is right on the long fault line that runs from Africa all the way into Turkey.

6. The city was burned with fire and this can still be seen by those who visit the site. There was a lot of charcoal and ash covering the ruins, and the walls were reddened by fire. The whole 1400 B.C. destruction strata is covered with a heavy layer of black ash.

7. This is the third archaeological team that had come to the same conclusion about the date. They found under the rubbish an abundance of wheat, barley, dates, and lentils that showed the conquerors did not salvage things, which is unusual for a destroyed city. They had obeyed the Lord who said Jericho was devoted to God as

the first fruits of their inheritance and, like the tithe, was to be given first back to God.

8. Israel had not had a payday for forty years. The Law of Moses said the first fruits of any harvest were to be given to God, not the last. This was to remind them where all blessings come from. The people had no new clothes or sandals, since they had not been able to go shopping or buy new clothing for forty years.

GOD PLACED A CURSE ON THE REBUILDER

In Joshua 6:26, God promised that a curse would fall on anyone who would rebuild the city.

"Joshua laid an oath on them at that time saying, 'At the cost of his firstborn shall he lay its foundation, and at the cost of his youngest son shall he set up its gates.'"

Excavation showed that the city of Jericho lay vacant from 1400 B.C. until the Ninth Century B.C. There was no sign of inhabitants for nearly 500 years. It was then rebuilt by Hiel. This account is found in I Kings 16:34.

"In his days Hiel of Bethel built Jericho. He laid its foundation at the cost of Abiram his firstborn, and set up its gates at the cost of his youngest son Segub, according to the word of the Lord, which he spoke by Joshua the son of Nun."

In the ruins of this Ninth Century rebuilding was found a large house, the nicest in the town; two large jars were found buried under the floor with the remains of two children. This may be tangible evidence of what I Kings had reported to have happened.

DR. CHARLES CRANE

The ancient city of Jericho was later abandoned and was replaced by a more modern city built by Herod the Great. This was about a mile distant, southwest of the ancient location. This city featured swimming pools and hot baths that were supplied by hot springs that are plentiful in the area.

This second location of Jericho was the place where Herod the Great died. As an old man he was eaten up by disease and was comforted by the nice weather and the hot spring baths.

According to Josephus, when Herod died the funeral procession reached from Jericho all the way to the Herodian where he was buried. This is about twenty miles. People came from all over the world to his funeral.

Modern Jericho is built all around the tel of Jericho and is a place of milk, fruit, vegetables, and honey. The winter temperature ranges from 70 to 80 degrees and there are many winter homes for the wealthy.

> Suggested Reading:
> Joshua 6
> Kenyon, Kathleen M., *The Bible and Recent Archaeology*.
> Blum, Howard, *The Gold of Exodus*.

Chapter Eleven

Ai and Gibeon

Ai

Israel came to their first dreadful defeat at Ai and Gibeon. This was because of the sin of Achan. He had taken things from Jericho that were to be devoted to God, and as a result, Israel had lost God's blessing. Coming right after the crossing of the Jordan in a miraculous way and the easy and miraculous defeat at Jericho, this defeat came as a fearful shock to Israel. Ai and Bethel were only one-and-one-half miles apart, both small villages and neither far from Gibeon.

God was with Israel, but He expected obedience to His commands. Joshua sent 3,000 soldiers to conquer Ai and they suffered a devastating defeat with 36 men killed (Joshua 7:2–5). The hearts of the people melted with fear. They were now in the midst of the enemy with no means of retreat because of the flooding Jordan, and they could not even defeat a small town.

Joshua tore his clothes and fell on the ground face first in prayer before the Ark of God. The elders put dust on their heads. Achan's sin was revealed and he and his family were put to death. All Achan owned was killed, burned, and buried under a huge stack of stones.

Even today, when men do not take the spiritual lead in their families, the result is often devastation to the man but unfortunately also to the whole family.

After dealing with Achan's sin, Joshua returned to Ai with 30,000 men and by ambush destroyed the city and killed the people. Some have questioned why God commanded that all of the Canaanites were to be killed. The land was a national Sodom and Gomorrah. Archaeology has shown that the people were infected with sexually transmitted diseases and also with sinful, idolatrous hearts. Baal, Asherah, and Moleck were central to their disgusting worship. Men, women, and children were infected. They had ample opportunity to know the true God, but had chosen to live by their lower sinful passions. Read Romans 1:18–23.

Not everyone was commanded to be killed but there were several tribes that were so evil God knew they would infect and ruin Israel if they remained in the land. Clean does not rub off on dirt, nor are godly people blessed by being with the ungodly.

The archaeological search for Ai has not produced very good results. There are several reasons. First, it was a small town and it was destroyed. Unlike Jericho, it was not an ancient village. Also making it difficult to identify is that under various conquerors it has had several different names. There has not remained enough of the place to positively identify it. It has no real archaeological value because of what happened there.

GIBEON

Joshua 9:1–15 tells about the five kings that came against Gibeon and Israel. God helped Israel by killing more of the enemy with huge hail stones than were killed by the warriors. The sun stood still almost an entire day, according to Joshua 10:12–14, helping Israel totally defeat these Canaanites.

BIBLICAL ARCHAEOLOGY

Ai, Bethel, and Gibeon are in the hilly country northeast of Jerusalem. This is a beautiful part of Israel with verdant forests, vineyards, olive orchards, and productive farms of grains and fruits. Here, as elsewhere in Israel, a town was dependent on a source of fresh water being nearby. Gibeon has such a water source.

After the defeat of Ai, Joshua assembled the people at Mt. Ebal, built an altar, and offered burnt offerings to the Lord. He then read from the farewell sermon of Moses about the blessings and cursings Moses promised, depending on whether they obeyed or disobeyed God. They would receive blessings if they obeyed God and cursing if they disobeyed (Deuteronomy 27—28). The blessings were read from Mt. Gerizim and curses from Mt. Ebal (evil). The town of Shechem lies between these hills. This is near Jacob's Well, which is still in use today and from which one can still get a cold drink of water.

The people of the whole land were terribly frightened by this victory and by the presence of Israel. Everyone in Canaan should have been afraid, as Israel had been followed by one miracle after another. There had been the crossing of the Red Sea, miracles of food and water provided in the wilderness, and now the crossing of Jordan at flood stage, and defeat of Jericho and Ai. The news had traveled far and near. The population consisted of many small city states, and without one unified government.

The men of Gibeon devised a plan to fool Joshua and make a covenant with Israel under false pretenses. They took old wineskins and filled them with wine and traveled to meet with Joshua at Gilgal (near Jericho) and told him they had come on a long journey. They said that when they left home the wineskins were new and now they were old. They said that the fame of Israel had reached their distant country and they had traveled a long way to make a peace treaty with Israel. Joshua did not consult God and made a hasty peace treaty with them.

The truth was that Gibeon was just across the hill from Ai, only about ten miles away. Both cities were in what would later become the land of Benjamin, which also included Jerusalem. Joshua honored the treaty, but because of their deception he made them wood cutters and water drawers for Israel and the altar of God (Joshua 9:27).

When the Canaanites learned about Gibeon's treaty with Israel, they rose up to punish Gibeon. Gibeon called upon Joshua to come to their defense, and he came. The battle was against several city states: Jerusalem, Hebron, Jarmuth, Lachish, and Eglon, who together marched against Gibeon.

THE SUN STOOD STILL AND HUGE HAIL

This led to the famous Battle of Gibeon in which the sun stood still for almost an entire day. God also threw down great hailstones from heaven against the Canaanites. The hail killed more than did Israel's soldiers (Joshua 10:12–14). This is reminiscent of the recent hail storm in Texas where the hail was the size of softballs.

Just how the sun and moon stood still we do not know. Some have conjectured that by a computer examination of the planetary system there is evidence of a missing day about this time. Frankly this seems rather farfetched, but not being a scientist or computer expert, the author is not qualified to judge. If the Bible says it, it happened. The God who created the whole universe should not have much trouble putting the rotation of the earth on pause for a few hours.

BIBLICAL ARCHAEOLOGY

FINDING GIBEON

Finding Gibeon has proved to be an almost insurmountable task for archaeologists. This is for some of the same reasons that Ai has been hard to find. It was ancient, had been destroyed and rebuilt, and occupied by different people groups over the years, which all added to the complexity of finding it. It is important archaeologically because several important biblical events happened here.

Gibeon, in Joshua's day, had been a major city, but the ebb and flow of history had left only a tel or ruins, which had borne other names over the centuries. Efforts over the years to identify it positively had been unproductive. This is no longer true.

The archaeologist James B. Pritchard said,

> We had just finished lunch when our chief pottery washer pulled a broken jar handle from his pocket. "I meant to show this to you earlier," he apologized. I glanced at it and forgot to reprove him. The fragment bore timeworn scratches—unmistakably four Hebrew letters: I read them, and all of the weeks of toil under a scorching sun faded from memory. The characters spelled Gibeon, the town of Biblical fame which our staff of nine and about a hundred laborers had been trying to find.
>
> "This handle speaks to us," was all I could say at the moment. In my fingers I held the autograph of the city where Joshua led the children of Israel to a great victory, calling on the Lord for time to complete his triumph: "Sun, stand thou still upon Gibeon" (Joshua 10:12). Here, "by the pool of Gibeon" (II Samuel 2:13), David's men clashed with Saul's. Here, "the Lord appeared to Solomon" and endowed him with "a wise and understanding heart" (I Kings 3:5, 12). Gibeon had been

found, and another archaeological link was forged between history, geography and our Holy Bible.

Under an olive tree, eight miles north of Jerusalem, Ibrahim the pottery washer and I were keeping a rendezvous in time with an unknown scribe of the seventh century B.C. This literate Gibeonite, a contemporary of Jeremiah the prophet, had inscribed a jar with a single word that enabled us to fit another stone into the arch that links us to the dim past.[29]

Before the evidence had pointed to this place as being Gibeon, but now it had been identified for sure. The stones and pottery have spoken out. Gibeon is now identified and excavated, bringing us very close to Joshua's battle, the sun standing still, and kings David and Solomon.

Gibeon is located at the modern village of El-Jib, six miles northwest of Jerusalem. Pottery and two Egyptian scarabs (stone beetles used as talismans, ornaments or symbols of resurrection, made in the likeness of small unisex beetles found in Egypt), indicate occupation of Gibeon at the time of the conquest by Joshua.

Gibeon was an important city, like one of the royal cities (Joshua 10:2). It ruled a small league of cities that included Kephirah, Beeroth and Kiriath, Jearim (Joshua 9:17). The Gibeonites traveled about 27 miles to Gilgal to meet with Joshua and under false pretenses made a treaty of peace with Israel.

There was another battle at Gibeon and it was between Ish-bosheth, the son of King Saul, and David and his followers.

---

29 *Archaeological Bible*, page 318.

BIBLICAL ARCHAEOLOGY

Abner, Saul's general, and Joab, David's general, met to settle whether Ish-bosheth or David was to rule Israel now that Saul was dead.

They met and the two groups were one on each side of the Pool of Gibeon. Twelve men were chosen from each side and they met in the area by the pool and grabbed each other by the beard and ran a knife through the other; all were killed. This began the Battle of Gibeon in which Joab and David's troops soundly defeated Abner. David lost 19 men that day and Abner lost 360. Eventually David succeeded in defeating the followers of Ish-bosheth (II Samuel 2:12–32).

What we can know about Gibeon:

1. Gibeonites were Hivites (Joshua 10:12 & 11:19).

2. Gibeon has been positively identified.

3. The archaeologist James Pritchard excavated there six times from 1956–1962.

4. It was a substantial city with finely crafted pottery, tombs, and a wine industry.

5. The pool of Gibeon has been found and it was inside the city walls. The water lies 80 feet below the ground level. There are two pools, one reached by 79 steps down, and 93 steps to the second. The pool itself is 22 x 11 feet. The pit reaching down to the pool averages 37 feet wide.

6. Proof of the wine industry is found in several wine cellars that would hold more than 95,000 liters of wine.

7. A pottery jar handle was found with the Hebrew word "Gibeon" inscribed on it.

8. Gibeon is mentioned on the wall of the temple of Amum at Karnak, Egypt celebrating the invasion of Israel and conquering of Gibeon by Pharaoh Shosheng in 945–924 B.C.

9. It became a Levitical city. This makes sense as Joshua made the Gibeonites servants of the altar of God (Joshua 21:17).[30]

Suggested Reading:
Halley's Bible Handbook
Everyday Life in Bible Times, National Geographic Society
The Archaeological Bible, Zondervan Publishing
Archaeological Commentary on the Bible, Doubleday
Wikipedia, on line.

---

30 This chapter is based on the author's personal travels and observation of this entire area of Israel over a period of more than forty years.

Chapter Twelve

Megiddo and Hazor

Megiddo is said to be the most important archaeological site found in all of Israel. (This may be true if you do not include Qumran and the Dead Sea Scrolls.) Megiddo is important to the Bible narrative from the time of Joshua, to Kings Solomon and Ahab, to the third century Christian era, the book of Revelation, and most of the wars of the world up through World War I. It is shockingly important to the study of history, knowing our Bibles, and is so impacting on our faith.

Megiddo is frequently mentioned in our Bible. Here are a few examples:

- Judges 1:27: "Manasseh did not drive out the inhabitants ... of Megiddo and its villages."

- Judges 5:19: "The kings came and they fought ... by the waters of Megiddo."

- I Kings 4:12 & 15: "And this is the account of the forced labor that King Solomon drafted to build ... Megiddo ..."

- II Kings 9:27: "Ahaziah ... fled to Megiddo and died there."

- II Kings 23:29–30: "... Josiah went to meet him and Pharaoh Neco killed him at Megiddo as soon as he saw him ... his servants carried him dead from Megiddo to Jerusalem and buried him."

- II Chronicles 35:22: Similar to II Kings ...

- Revelation 16:16: "And they assembled them at the place that in Hebrew is called Armageddon."

MEGIDDO, THE MEANING OF THE NAME

In Greek, Hebrew, Latin, and Assyrian, the name is similar enough to be recognized as Megiddo.

In Hebrew it is called Armageddon from the Hebrew "Har Megiddo," or Mount of Megiddo or Armageddon. Armageddon is falsely associated with the end of the world and the great final battle. Even a casual reading of the text of Revelation chapter 16 shows that it is the sixth battle of seven, not the great and final one. Associating Armageddon with the end of the world is a false understanding. A lot happens on earth after Armageddon according to the book of Revelation.

HISTORY OF MEGIDDO

Megiddo was valued for its strategic position on the Via Maris, or sea road. It was one of the main routes between Egypt, Syria, Mesopotamia, and Europe. There was also the King's Highway inland, but the Via Maris was the main road along the sea, turning inland near Megiddo.

Megiddo was first inhabited in the 20th Century B.C., not long after the Flood of Noah and the Tower of Babel. It became a fortified city state, and the headquarters for the surrounding area and villages. It was heavily fortified.

BIBLICAL ARCHAEOLOGY

In Joshua's time it was inhabited by Canaanites and later was controlled and modernized by King Solomon and later King Ahab. Israel's connection with Megiddo was broken by the Assyrian invasion and capture of the ten northern tribes of Israel. Megiddo was destroyed and rebuilt many times. In time it declined in importance as a city, but the fort remained an important area for world events because of its strategic location.

It can almost be said for certain that all the armies that came to Israel came here. Ebla, Assyria, Babylon, Egypt, General Alexander the Great, and General Allenby came or fought battles here. The Greeks, Romans, Muslims, Crusaders, Mamlukes, Mongols, Persians, French, Ottomans, British, Germans, Arabs, and Israelites have all fought here. It is probably the most blood-soaked spot on earth. It was the place where British General Edmund Allenby launched the attack on the Turks in 1917, a pivotal battle in bringing an end to World War I.

Many interesting things have been found here, or near here. One finding has been called "Solomon's Stables" but may in fact have been built by King Ahab. These are chariot stables, with remaining pillars where the horses were tied and troughs where they would have been fed and watered.

A huge grain silo has been found that probably dates to the time of King Jeroboam in the 8th century B.C., possibly earlier. A large and ornate altar has been uncovered. Its use is not certainly known. Some have suggested human sacrifices were offered here; if not, it may have been a place of sacrifice for one of the pagan deities.

THE WATER SYSTEM

Water has always been a vital issue to life and security in Israel. This has been true from ancient times even until our

DR. CHARLES CRANE

own day. Megiddo has an ingenious water system devised so people did not have to go outside the walls to get water in the frequent times of battle or danger.

Early in Megiddo's history the water source was outside the walls, and running from the hill close by. A vertical shaft was sunk 120 feet deep inside the walls, going down 183 steps. This vertical hole met a 215-foot horizontal tunnel that reached the water source, bringing the water inside the walls. The outside exit for the water was plugged up and obscured so that it looked like part of the hill upon which Megiddo was built.

Today the farming area that surrounds Megiddo has many wells that supply water for their crops. These are heavily pumped. This has lowered the water table so that the spring is normally dried up except in periods when there is a lot of rain.

One feature of the ancient water systems has puzzled archaeologists. How could these underground water shafts be dug through solid rock and reach the desired location? Some of them were dug from both ends meeting in the middle. Often the shafts were hundreds of feet long.

James Michener, in his book *The Source*, has a resident, "Hoopoe," design the process here at Megiddo to dig the 215- foot underground water shaft. He said engineer Hoopoe put an arrow mounted on the earth's surface, pointing the direction the shaft was to go. At the bottom of the vertical shaft another arrow pointed the same direction as the one above on the surface. They would sight down this arrow to know the direction they should dig. Arrows could point from both ends of the dig so they would meet in the middle.

BIBLICAL ARCHAEOLOGY

JAMES MICHENER AND HIS BOOK THE SOURCE

This leads us to James Michener, who is primarily a historian and has written many books about important historical places and events. His histories are normally quite accurate. He has written a history of Israel that he calls *The Source*. The Hebrew word for source is "Macor." So he writes his history around a fortified city called Macor. In reality he is writing about Megiddo, which he has renamed Macor in his historical novel.

He begins his story in prehistoric times. He dates these events much earlier than is realistic, as we have learned that no pre-flood cities have been found. Megiddo thus had its beginning after the Tower of Babel and probably by Canaan the son of Ham. The earliest people living along the Mediterranean coast lived in caves at the base of Mt. Carmel. The earliest evidence of civilization in Canaan has been found there.

After the flood and as population grew, travel between Africa and Europe passed by Megiddo. Megiddo became an important way point for supplies and to oversee and protect the area from bandits and invaders. It became one of the most important fortresses in Israel. There was a constant flow of traffic of people and armies. The road passed through a valley from the coast inland and past Megiddo, on to Hazor, and further to the north on the road to Damascus and points in Europe.

TEL MEGIDDO

There are at least twenty cities built one on top of another here. The archaeological excavations have found temples, lavish palaces, massive fortifications, private homes, large places to store food, a huge grain silo, and, as has already been mentioned, an elaborately engineered water system. The main gate to the city had a place for meeting. It was designed with a sharp curve in the roadway so incoming traffic had to slow to a snail's pace to enter. This forced fast-moving traffic to slow to a crawl so horses and chariots could not rush in, making it easier to defend. In early cities in Israel, most of the business was transacted at the city gate. Such appears to be the case here.

Megiddo was almost continuously inhabited from just after the Tower of Babel until about 500 years before Christ, when it declined in importance but continued to be inhabited.

Its strategic position at a pass through the Carmel Mountains caused it to dominate this ancient trade and military route for centuries. This assured its financial prosperity and importance. Anyone going through the area had to pass through and pay the toll, and they could also restock supplies as they headed north or south into desolate regions. The world passed by their doors.

A very significant find here was a 3rd Century A.D. Christian prayer hall. It is probably the most ancient church discovered in all of Israel. A mosaic inscription reads, "God Jesus Christ." This helps us understand the 3rd Century church's view of who Jesus was.

THE TRUE AND UNTRUE

Megiddo has had more fictional and ridiculous things written about it than probably any other spot on earth. These stories include science fiction, horror books, movies, and most egregious of all, the end-time events prophecies. These oft times ill-informed "theologians" often show their misunderstanding of history, the Bible, and biblical prophecy. These writings and films do make fascinating reading and watching but should not be considered factual, as mostly they are not. [31]

BIBLICAL ARCHAEOLOGY

TEL HAZOR

Tel Hazor is in upper Galilee, north of the Sea of Galilee in the Hula Valley and overlooking what was Lake Merom, now drained and turned into farm land.

Around 1750 B.C. and later in the Israelite period of the ninth century B.C. it was the largest fortified city in the country and one of the most important in the Fertile Crescent. It maintained commercial ties with Babylon and Syria. Hazor imported lots of tin to be used in their bronze industry.

In the Book of Joshua it is described as "the head of all these kingdoms" (Joshua 11:10). This probably refers to its importance in Northern Palestine.

Yigal Yadin, in the mid-1950s led the dig of Hazor which was one of the most important of Israel's early years of statehood. It is the largest archaeological site in Northern Israel. The upper tel is 30 acres and lower city 175, for a total of over 200 acres.

According to the book of Joshua, Jabin was a powerful Canaanite king at Hazor and he led a confederation against Joshua and was defeated by Joshua, who burned Hazor to the ground. This destruction has been confirmed by excavation.

Hazor appears in other biblical narratives, with another Jabin ruling there in the time of the Judges.

Hazor was a guard station for Northern Palestine and Israel and on important trade routes from north, south, east and west.

---

31   Based in part on the author's research and his many visits to Megiddo over more than forty years.

DR. CHARLES CRANE

It was on a main route to another important city, Damascus, the oldest continually inhabited city in this part of the world.

Hazor also had an interesting water system, but not as elaborate as the one at Megiddo. Additional research of Hazor is a good investment of time. It is suggested that the reader Google Hazor, Israel.

Suggested Reading:
Halley's Bible Handbook
The Archaeology Bible
The Bible & Recent Archaeology, Kathleen M. Kenyon
Biblical Archaeology Review
Internet sources
The Source, James Michener

Chapter Thirteen

Writings, Inscriptions, and Languages

COULD ADAM AND EVE READ AND WRITE?

Questions have been raised about the early Bible histories and whether those who left these records could actually read and write. Some have suggested that the early biblical records were handed down as legends, but not in a written form. Archaeologists have helped clear up these questions. They have found documents that prove that people could read and write very early in human history, if not back to the beginning.

According to Genesis 2:19–20, Adam was instructed to name everything, which meant he could talk, had a language, and needed to make a list of the thousands of things he named. It stands to reason he could read and write. How else could he have named everything and recorded these names?

John Rawls, (the author's Hebrew professor at Lincoln Christian Seminary) was an expert in Middle Eastern languages. He could read and write eleven Semitic languages, as well as Greek and German. In class he would affirm that Hebrew was the language that God taught Adam and Eve. That is certainly open to debate. But that Adam and Eve had a well-defined spoken language is not debatable as they walked and talked with God. It is quite probable that they could write, as well.

Hebrew tradition affirms that Adam wrote down the creation account, and passed it on to Methuselah, who gave this record to Noah, who took it on the ark during the flood. The people's lives from Adam to Methuselah and Noah generationally did overlap. This may be a bit of conjecture, but does have a ring of credibility. Very ancient tradition does say that there was a recorded history of mankind. If there was this record, taking it on the ark would have been important.

Of course, God used inspiration to guide Moses and the writers of our Bible books. He revealed many important things to Moses and adding to this list the history of creation would have been no problem. But archaeological information, now in our hands, indicates that people spoke and wrote as far back as history can be traced. They not only wrote, they wrote very well and in eloquent literary styles.

This chapter will not examine ancient writings necessarily in chronological order, nor order of significance, but will make a brief review of some of the most exciting finds among ancient written documents which have survived.

THE BEHISTUN ROCK

The Behistun Rock made it possible to decipher the ancient Babylonian language, which before could not be read. In 1835 Sir Henry Rawlinson, a British army officer stationed in Persia, noticed on Behistun mountain, 200 miles northeast of Babylon, on the road to Ecbatana, at the border of Media, a great isolated rock. It was a rising perpendicular cliff that rose 1,700 feet above the plain. Four hundred feet above the road, was a smoothed surface with carvings on it.

He investigated and found an engraved inscription by the order of King Darius about 516 B.C. Darius was king of Persia from 521–485 B.C. This is the same Darius under whom the

Temple in Jerusalem was rebuilt, as recorded in the book of Ezra. This inscription on the rock was engraved the same year as the Temple in Jerusalem was rebuilt.

The inscription was in three languages—Persian, Elamite, and Babylonian. It told of the conquests of Darius and the glories of his reign. Rawlinson had some knowledge of the Persian language and assumed that it was the same inscription in three different languages.

With amazing perseverance over a four year period, and in constant risk of his life, he climbed the rock and stood on a ledge about a foot wide at the bottom of the inscriptions to examine them. With the aid of ladders from below, and swings let down from above, he made squeezes of the inscriptions.

It took him 14 years to complete his translations, but he found the key to the ancient Babylonian language by comparing the same story told in three different languages. By so doing he unlocked to the world the vast treasures of ancient Babylonian literature.[32]

THE ROSETTA STONE

In 1799, a soldier's spade helped loose the ancient Egyptian tongue. Engineers of Napoleon's army dug for a foundation for a fort near Rosetta on the Nile Delta. One soldier struck an ancient slab inscribed in priestly hieroglyphic, in everyday demotic, and in the Greek tongue of the Ptolemies who ruled Egypt just before Jesus' day. Scholars easily read the Greek. It lauded a teenaged Ptolemy V (Epiphanes) who ruled from 203–181 B.C.

---

32 This is a brief summary from *Halley's Bible Handbook*, page 43.

With the same story told in three languages and thus guided, they groped for the meaning of the hieroglyphic symbols, and the shorthand-like jots of demotic, found on the famed "Rosetta Stone." Not until 1822 did French scholar and boy genius Champollion unlock the scripts and quicken the newborn science of Egyptology.

The author has seen the Rosetta Stone in the British Museum, in London, England. Although not as ancient as other finds, it is very significant since it opened much of the ancient Egyptian records for us today. We will discuss more about this important find later.[33]

THE AMARNA TABLETS AND THE HABIRU

A few decades after the conquest of Canaan by the Israelites, a reformer and visionary pharaoh came to the throne in Egypt. His name was Amenhotep IV. He built a new capital in Amarna which he called Akhetaten, about 250 miles north of the original capital at Thebes. After his 17-year reign the capital was moved back to Thebes.

In 1887 a Bedouin woman discovered a number of clay tablets with writing on them among the ruins of Akhetaten. When it was discovered that these tablets were valuable, the local natives dug up hundreds of them and sold them to museums. Some more were found by sanctioned excavations which helped preserve them.

These tablets are written in Akkadian (Babylonian) script, instead of Egyptian hieroglyphics. They cover a period of about 20 years during the mid-14th century B.C. Some of these letters are outgoing mail, but most are incoming, telling

---

33 *Everyday Life in Bible Times*, National Geographic Society, page 22.

of events in the Near Middle East, including Canaan.

The letters from Canaan provide a rare look at the conditions fifty years after Israel left Egypt. The Canaanites complained about the Habiru who had infiltrated the urbanized areas and were troublesome to the metropolitan populations. It is quite possible that these Habiru were in fact the Hebrews. This would be confirmation of the biblical accounts that took place during our books of Joshua and Judges.

EXAMPLES OF ANCIENT WRITING

Following are pictures of some of the most important written documents with a brief explanation of what they contain. Notice how they relate to the Bible record. The narrative about each has a Bible book and chapter listed that relates to how they support the biblical record.[34]

THE ROSETTA STONE

Exodus 9

The Rosetta Stone is in the British Museum and made it possible to decipher Hieroglyphs.

Known as the Rosetta Stone, this stele helped to solve the mystery of the Egyptian writing system known as hieroglyphics, thereby providing the key to understanding much of Egyptian history and culture recorded on ancient monuments and tablets.

---

34 The following pictures are copied from a book written by Dr. James C. Martin, *Preserving Bible Times*, and he shows the pictures by permission of the various museums where they are kept.

Originally inscribed to honor Ptolemy V Epiphanes (203–181 B.C.) this stone is divided into three sections called registers, each of which contains the same text but in a different writing system, hieroglyphics, demotic and Greek. At the time of its discovery only the bottom, Greek register could be read.

The most exciting breakthrough in decoding the hieroglyphics occurred when a young historian and language genius named J.F. Campollion realized that the writing included symbols not only for letters but also for syllable-like sounds and even for entire words. Champollion solved this riddle substantially in 1822 which has made it possible to read hieroglyphics.

THE LAWS OF ESHNUNNA

Deuteronomy 9

The city of Eshnunna lies east of Babylon and for a brief period, about 1800 B.C., was a dominant city in Mesopotamia and a code of laws has been discovered there. It appears that King Dadusha was a successor of Narma-Sin who was the founder of the dynasty. King Dadusha issued this law code for his city.

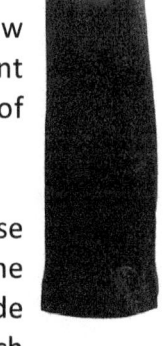

This is the earliest example of an Akkadian law code found so far. It is similar in form and content to its successor, the much more famous Code of Hammurabi.

This stele shows that a code of laws similar to those we find in the Bible existed much earlier than the time of Moses. Some have argued that Moses' law code must have come at a later date than Moses, since such

BIBLICAL ARCHAEOLOGY

advanced thinking had not yet developed. This picture is of the Code of Hammurabi and is found in the Louvre in Paris.

BABYLON

Isaiah 13

Babylon was one of the greatest cities of ancient Mesopotamia. It was an important city as early as 2100 B.C. reaching back to the time of the Tower of Babel, not long after the flood of Noah. It became the hub of Old Babylon under Hammurabi (1792–1750 B.C.) Outside the walls of Babylon was a moat fed by the Euphrates River ranging in width from 60–250 feet. Here we have a picture of Hammurabi of Babylon. This stele is found in the British Museum in London.

HAMMURABI

Deuteronomy 12

Hammurabi, sometimes called Hammurapi, was the sixth king of the first dynasty of Babylon. He ruled approximately in the eighteenth century B.C., and was a vigorous and successful king. His fame has been brought about because of the wide fame of his law code called The Code of Hammurabi. He made large steles and placed them near the entrances to cities he controlled.

He appears to have been harsh and arbitrary, but not a total tyrant. His code followed a pattern found earlier and previously mentioned. These steles served to remind the people of his authority over his domain. Here is the top of the stele of the Code of

Hammurabi and shows the sun-god Shamash seated giving Hammurabi the symbols of power. This is found in the Louvre in Paris.

LANGUAGES OF THE OLD TESTAMENT WORLD

Ezra 2

Here are three examples of writing from the Old Testament period. The first is an administrative letter addressed to Hammurabi. (The ancient Near East had several different languages such as Egyptian, Akkadian, Ugaritic, Aramaic and Hebrew, of which there are eleven or more in number.)

The second shows an early pictographic writing from Upper Egypt, from the third century B.C. The third shows us hieroglyphic writing.

AKKADIAN DIVINATION

Deuteronomy 18:9-14

The Law of Moses prohibited the Israelites from making use of diviners and sorcerers who engaged in detestable practices. Israel was not to be like other nations. There were several common practices such as reading

 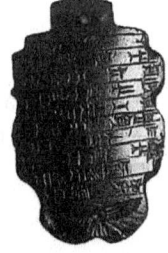

BIBLICAL ARCHAEOLOGY

animal entrails, the observation of patterns in oil dropped on water and dream interpretations.

If a drop of oil spilled on water split in two, a sick individual would die or an army would fail to return from battle. If a person dreamed about a dog ripping his or her clothing, that individual was in for a financial loss. A black cat in someone's house was a sign of good fortune. Here we have two Assyrian incantation texts and they come from about 900–600 B.C. From the Scheyen Collection.

THE AMARNA TABLETS AND THE HABIRU

Judges 2

A few decades after the conquest of Israel in the mid-fourteenth century B.C., a reformer and visionary named Amenhotep IV came to the throne in Egypt. He brought about many changes.

In 1887 a Bedouin woman discovered a number of clay tablets with writing on them among the ruins of Akhetaten. When it was learned they were valuable many other looked for these tablets. Many were found. These tablets were in the Akkadian or Babylonian language of the day instead of Egyptian hieroglyphics. These tablets span a period of about 20 years, during Akhetaten's reign and during the mid-fourteenth to twelfth century B.C.

These tablets reported that there were hostilities among the small city states in Canaan; in particular they complained about a group of people called Habiru. If the pharaoh did not take action, the letter warned that all of Canaan would be taken over by these people. One tablet said, "The war against me is severe ... Habiru have plundered all the lands of the king." These Habiru are mentioned in several other ancient texts. This tablet is in the Cairo Museum, Egypt.

THE DESCENT OF ISHTAR

Judges 6

Christians today may find it hard to see how Israelites could so quickly turn from God to idols or pagan gods. It is helpful to see how widespread and accepted these pagan gods and practices were. A possible explanation for people's quick defection was that these religions appealed to people's lower nature. This tablet is a hymn to Inanna or Ishtar and comes from the period of the twentieth to seventeenth century B.C. This is from the Scheyen Collection.

THE MERNEPTAH STELE

Judges 8

The Merneptah Stele is an inscribed stone slab discovered in Pharoah Mernepthah's mortuary temple in Thebes, Egypt in 1896. This monument is the earliest record of Israel outside the Bible and contains one of only two such references of Israel in Egyptian records, outside the Bible. Another is found at Memphis and is a large monument speaking of Israel in Goshen.

As often is the case, this stele exaggerates Mernepthah's accomplishments. He did not annihilate Israel as the stele implies. Israel is among the city states and nations supposedly defeated by this pharaoh. It shows that Israel was an important entity or he would not boast about defeating them.

BIBLICAL ARCHAEOLOGY

This stele demonstrates that Israel was a recognized people around 1200 B.C. It provides us with an outside boundary for fixing the date of the exodus and conquest. Israel was already in the land and well established by 1150 B.C. The Merneptah Stele is in the Cairo Museum in Egypt.

THE MOABITE (MESHA) STONE

II Kings 3

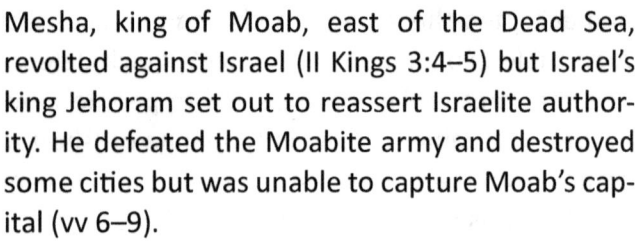

Mesha, king of Moab, east of the Dead Sea, revolted against Israel (II Kings 3:4–5) but Israel's king Jehoram set out to reassert Israelite authority. He defeated the Moabite army and destroyed some cities but was unable to capture Moab's capital (vv 6–9).

A unique discovery made in Dhiban, Jordan, in 1868 describes Mesha's revolt from the Moabite perspective. It mentions Yahweh the God of Israel. The Old Testament says that Mesha raised sheep and this is corroborated by a statement by Mesha saying he brought flocks to the house of Baal Meon. (Baal was one of the detestable gods that, was among other things, devoted to sexual depravity.) Twelve other Moabite towns are mentioned in this inscription. These same towns are described in the Bible (Isaiah 15, Jeremiah 48, and Ezekiel 25). The Moabite Stone resides in the Louvre in Paris.

THE HISTORY OF THE SOUTHERN KINGDOM

II Kings 7

Israel divided after the death of King Solomon. The southern two tribes were Judah and Benjamin that were called Judah. David's descendants ruled here until the Babylonian captivity. Twenty kings ruled for a period of 345 years.

These two stone fragments were found at Tel Dan and tell about "The House of David." These are the only artifacts found so far that talk about David's house. These fragments reside in the Israel Museum in Jerusalem.

THE SENNACHERIB CYLINDER

II Kings 19

In II Kings 19:5–7, the prophet Isaiah foretold that the Lord would deliver Jerusalem from the hand of the Assyrian king Sennacherib (704–681 B.C.) who was besieging Jerusalem. Isaiah predicted that Sennacherib would hear a report and return to his own land to be killed by the sword. 185,000 of his soldiers died by the plague and his forces were so depleted he had to return home where he was killed by his sons Adrammelech and Sharezer while praying in the temple of Nisroch. This multisided stone inscription describes Sennacherib's campaigns and the rebuilding of Nineveh. This is found in the British Museum in London.

THE SEAL OF MANASSEH

II Kings 21

Manasseh became king when he was only 12 years old and ruled for 55 years (II Kings 21:1; 697–642 B.C.) During this time

BIBLICAL ARCHAEOLOGY

Judah was defiled by idolatry, child sacrifice and witchcraft. Manasseh was punished by God and was taken by Assyria and they imprisoned him in Babylon. He repented and was returned to Jerusalem where he initiated building programs and religious reforms.

Manasseh's name has been found in three other documents about the same period as the Manasseh seal. This inscription describes the conquest of Ashurbanipal and is in the British Museum in London.

SUMERIAN SCRIBAL EDUCATION

I Chronicles 2

In the ancient world scribes held a position of high prestige like our attorneys or accountants today. Select young men attended scribal schools to learn the trade. Several pieces of Old Babylonian literature tell us about Mesopotamian scribal schools. During their training older students who were called "big brothers" helped tutor the younger to learn their lessons and skills.

These scribes mastered their language, sometimes others, as well as signs, mathematics, weights and measures, budgeting and business management. They learned how to write contracts and to meticulously and accurately copy important documents. Levites, as keepers of the biblical texts, appear to have served as scribes along with their other duties. Here we have an Akkadian lexical tablet showing synonyms, a tool for the use of the scribes. This tablet is in the British Museum in London.

RABBAH

I Chronicles 20

Rabbah was the Ammonite capital, situated along the King's Highway at edge of the desert and controlled north-south commerce in ancient times. An excavation near the site of the Amman airport found tablets that suggest that Hittites were there during the fourteenth and thirteenth centuries B.C.

This cylinder from the time of Nebuchadnezzar II talks of Rabbah. This is where the iron bed of Og of Bashan was located. Centuries later David conquered the city after its king had humiliated his ambassadors by cutting off half of their beards and hair. It was at Rabbah that David had Uriah the Hittite killed in battle so he could have Bathsheba as his wife. This cylinder is in the Israel museum at Jerusalem.

THE SIPPAR CYLINDER OF NABONIDUS

II Chronicles 36

The conclusion of Chronicles describes the destruction of Jerusalem and the exile of the Judahites under Nebuchadnezzar in 586 B.C. The exiles served Nebuchadnezzar and his successors until the kingdom of Persia came to power (II Chronicles 36:20). At that time Cyrus conquered Babylon and let the Jews return to their homeland and helped reinstate them there (II Chronicles 36:22–23). This cylinder talks of the ending of Nabonidus' reign and ascendency of the Persian Empire. The Sippar Cylinder is in the British Museum in London.

BIBLICAL ARCHAEOLOGY

THE CYRUS CYLINDER

Ezra 6

When work on the temple resumed in 520 B.C., the Persian governor Tattenai requested a search for the decree Cyrus had issued in 538 B.C. authorizing the Jews to rebuild their temple (Ezra 5:6—6:1). The Cyrus Cylinder is an inscription on a clay barrel discovered in Babylon in 1879 and documents Cyrus's policy of religious tolerance and liberation.

Cyrus bragged about this action, saying that he was beloved of the gods because of his actions. In fact, Cyrus was determined to be a benevolent rather than a heavy-handed ruler. He returned stolen images to their sanctuaries and in his own words, "gathered all their inhabitants and returned them to their dwellings." The Cyrus Cylinder is in the British Museum in London.

THE SCRIBE

Ezra 8

As already indicated, scribes had an important place in ancient civilizations. They were of a very high professional class in society. The scribal arts of reading, writing, and interpreting written documents assured them a vital role in the affairs of persons, state, and sanctuary. They used a stylus, reed, or pen and transcribed documents or took dictation.

Scribes are often mentioned in scripture, both Old and New Testaments. Men like Shaphan, Baruch, and Ezra are mentioned and even the New Testament writer Matthew used his scribal skills to record the first gospel book (Matthew 8:19; 13:52). Here we have an image of an Egyptian scribe and a lexical list of temples. Their location is uncertain.

BAAL TEXT

Psalm 104

Baal was one of the three main pagan gods of Canaan that were a constant cause of sin and evil in Israel. This two-piece tablet was discovered at the site of Ras Shamra, which is ancient Ugarit. The Myth of Baal is one of the longest literary works of the wester Semitic peoples in the second millennium B.C. This text describes the conflict between Baal and other gods, in which Baal wins. Baal was a part of the fertility cycle, with Baal seasonally "disappearing" from the earth.

Psalm 104 is a creation psalm that uses some of the imagery possibly known from the Myth of Baal. God, of course, is more powerful than any pagan god. The Ugaritic text of the Myth of Baal is located in the Louvre in Paris.

THE GEZER CALENDAR

Psalm 107

This calendar was found at Gezer, between Israel and Philistia. Gezer lies in the low hills that separate Israel and Philistia. The place where it was found (Gezer) today is called Tel Jezer. Gezer was on the Via Maris, or "Way of the

BIBLICAL ARCHAEOLOGY

Sea," an important north-south road. This stone was found in 1908.

Scholars have used this brief text to try to better understand Israelite agricultural practices. It suggests that the planting of grains began in October, after the rains had softened the soil to allow for plowing. Grain sowing lasted for two months, followed by two months of vegetable sowing. After a month of hoeing, the harvest began in the spring with first the barley, then the wheat, then the grapes, and finally the summer fruit. The text of the calendar has also proved important in the study of early Hebrew spelling and the development of the shapes of letters. The Gezer Calendar is in the Istanbul Archaeological Museum.

BOUNDARY MARKER or THE TEACHING OF AMENEMOPE

Proverbs 22

There are similarities between Proverbs and the teachings of Amenemope which is on papyrus and comes from the time of Rameses. It is preserved complete and is in the British Museum, along with other fragments. Amenemope instructs his young son in the proper conduct for a young man, who is to be contented, confidential, self-controlled, conciliatory towards his superiors, and honoring to his god.

Pictured here is a boundary marker stone found at Babylon. This stone dates to 1100 B.C. This helps us understand that property ownership is very ancient. This stone is found in the British Museum in London.

DR. CHARLES CRANE

EPIC OF GILGAMESH

Ecclesiastes 9

One of the longest literary compositions known from Mesopotamia is the Epic of Gilgamesh. The tale is of an ancient king's failed quest for immortality. It is a very old work, dating to about 2000 B.C. The result learned from the king's search was to eat, drink, delight in one's children, and provide joy for one's wife.

Scholars have noted the similarity of this to the advice given in Ecclesiastes 9:3, 7–10; 11:7—12:1. It is conjectured that the writer of Ecclesiastes knew about and appreciated this earlier work of Gilgamesh when he wrote. Both works wrestle with the question  of how one should live their lives when life seems to make no sense. Gilgamesh and the Bull of Heaven; come from early second millennium B.C. This comes from the Scheyen Collection.

SARGON II CYLINDER

Isaiah 10

Sargon is mentioned in scripture and his existence is confirmed by these two artifacts. The first is a prism inscription of Sargon II and the second of a winged androcephalus from the Palace of Sargon II. Again we have confirmation of the historical accuracy of our Bible. These are located in the Israel Museum in Jerusalem.

BIBLICAL ARCHAEOLOGY

BUSINESS RECEIPTS

Isaiah 30

Preserved ancient writing is commonly on clay tablets, either sun baked or fired. Isaiah 30:8 refers to this practice. Here we have a cuneiform receipt for the purchase of three oxen, about 2046 B.C. and a very early pictographic script from Sumer. Both are good examples of the many clay tablets that have been found. These two items are in the British Museum in London.

OLDEST SIGNATURE – The Eunuch

Isaiah 56

The Bible refers to the eunuch in Isaiah 56:3–5, which can be best understood in the light of Deuteronomy 23:1 which forbade eunuchs from entering the assembly of the Lord. The Hebrew word is "saris" which has the meaning of one by the side of the king, or "castrated official." Early Bible use of the word meant official, not necessarily eunuch. Here is a list of titles and professions and on the reverse is the earliest known signature. This dates to the early second or late third century B.C. From the Scheyen collection.

SECOND CENTURY B.C. PAPYRUS OF THE SEPTUAGINT

Here is the earliest known papyrus copy of the Septuagint which comes from the second century B.C. The Old Testament was mostly written in Hebrew. But in the second and third century B.C. it was translated into Greek. This translation is called the Septuagint. Some believe the Septuagint is more accurate than the Hebrew, because of its very early date. In reality both have great value since they are essentially the same. With the finding of the Dead Sea Scrolls we have very accurate texts that mostly  date before the birth of Christ. This very early fragment from Jeremiah is additional proof of the antiquity and accuracy of our Bible book of Jeremiah. This fragment is owned by the Jerusalem Bible Society, Israel.

ANCIENT FLOOD STORIES

Psalm 89

About three hundred ancient flood stories have been found from civilizations around the world, including the Native Americans. In the Bible the flood account is primarily found in Genesis. There are other accounts that help us see how the ancient Israelites viewed creation. An example of this is found in Psalm 89.

Other ancient texts in Akkadian, as well as hieroglyphics, have been found telling about creation. These flood accounts have been found at Ebla, Nineveh, and Babylon. Here is a cuneiform tablet containing one of the ancient flood accounts. This tablet is dated in the period between 750–200 B.C. This tablet is housed in the British Museum in Jerusalem.[35]

---

35 For a great deal of additional information about the Bible and archaeological findings a good resource is the *Archaeological Bible* that is done by Dr. Duane A. Garrett, professor of Old Testament at Gordon-Conwell Theological

BIBLICAL ARCHAEOLOGY

Here is what we have learned from ancient writings and inscriptions that confirms the biblical record.

1. That writing goes back into the dim and distant past. It is fallacious to suggest that people could not read and write, almost certainly they wrote clear back to creation and Adam and Eve. The evidence points to writing as far back as we have evidence of civilization.

2. The evidence indicates that these ancient people were very brilliant and their knowledge was of many difficult subjects, many of which are still understood only by the most learned people today.

3. The Bible narrative and history is supported time after time by ancient documents.

4. The nations, peoples, and rulers mentioned in the Bible were real people and there is a lot of evidence, outside the Bible, of who they were and what they did.

5. The Bible stands every test we give it. It stands alone among all of the writings of mankind as an inspired book (II Timothy 3:16–17 and John 10:35).[36]

Seminary. This work is printed by Zondervan Publishing. This work has been referenced for this chapter. This *Archaeological Bible* can be purchased at most Christian book stores or other major retailers of books.

36 The author has seen many of these ancient writings in the various museums where they are kept.

DR. CHARLES CRANE

THE ANVIL OF GOD'S WORD

Last eve I stood beside the blacksmith's door,
    And heard the anvil ring the vesper chimes,
    Then looking in, I saw upon the floor,
    Old hammers worn by beating years of time.

"How many anvils have you had" said I
    "To wear and batter all these hammers so?"
"Just one", said he, and then with twinkling eye,
    "The anvil wears out the hammers, you know."

"And so," I thought, "the anvil of God's word,
    For ages skeptic blows have beat upon,
Yet, though the noise of falling blows was heard,
    The Anvil is unharmed, the hammers gone."
            John Clifford, D.D.

Suggested Reading:
Halley's Bible Handbook
Everyday Life in Bible Times, National Geographic Society
The Archaeological Bible, Zondervan
Preserving Bible Times
The Internet
Biblical Archaeology Review, 1976–2012

Chapter Fourteen

Jerusalem

Our archaeological journey now takes us to Jerusalem and events that happened there or near there. In this chapter we will examine the following:

- The Gihon Spring, Warren's Shaft, and Hezekiah's Tunnel

- Solomon's and Nehemiah's walls

- The courtyard of the Praetorium Guard

- The High Priest's house and pit

- The Garden of Gethsemane

- Calvary and

- The Garden Tomb

THE ANCIENT HISTORY OF JERUSALEM

The date when Jerusalem was founded is open to discussion. Ancient dating is not an exact science. Although some say Jerusalem was founded 2800 B.C., or earlier, it is probable that the date was 2300–2200 B.C. Nevertheless it was a long time ago and Jerusalem is among the most ancient cities on earth. It may have been settled by the Canaanites and from Ham's family.

The Amarna letters give us the first record of its existence and that was in the 14th century B.C. Another early mention is in Genesis when Abraham met Melchizedek there after his battle with the Kings who captured Lot (Genesis 14:17–20). The place is there called "Salem" but is almost certainly Jerusalem.

When the land was divided among the tribes, Jerusalem was in the area allotted to the tribe of Benjamin, just north of Judah. During Israel's rule of Palestine it was the largest city.

Jerusalem is a tel, like many of the other cities we have studied. There have been several cities built one on top of the other. Some areas of Jerusalem still remain on bedrock, such as the Temple Mount.

David captured Jerusalem after reigning seven-and-one-half years from Hebron.

> At Hebron he reigned over Judah seven years and six months, and at Jerusalem he reigned over all Israel and Judah thirty-three years. And the king and his men went to Jerusalem against the Jebusites, the inhabitants of the land, who said to David, "You will not come in here, but the blind and the lame will ward you off"—thinking, "David cannot come in here." Nevertheless, David took the stronghold of Zion, that is, the city of David. And David said on that day, "Whoever would strike the Jebusites, let him get up the water shaft to attack the lame and the blind, who are hated by David's soul." Therefore it is said, "The blind and the lame shall not come into the house." And David lived in the stronghold and called it the city of David. And David built the city all around from the Millo inward.

BIBLICAL ARCHAEOLOGY

And David became greater and greater, for the Lord, the God of hosts, was with him (II Samuel 5:5–10).

David and his valiant men entered through the Gihon water shaft and straight up about 55 feet through a hole in the rock. Just how they did this must have required some serious planning.

David captured Jerusalem about 1000 B.C. and ruled there until about 970 B.C. David bought a place of sacrifice, from Araunah, for fifty pieces of silver as a place for him to offer sacrifices (II Samuel 24:18–25). This is the location where Solomon's Temple was later built.

After the Babylonian captivity, Nehemiah rebuilt the temple that had been destroyed by Nebuchadnezzar. Later Herod the Great built his temple there. This is where the Dome of the Rock Mosque stands today.

Nebuchadnezzar destroyed Solomon's Temple in 586 B.C. After the Jews spent seventy years of captivity in Babylon, Cyrus the Great permitted the first Jews to return to Israel in 516 B.C. when their 70 years of exile, predicted by Jeremiah, were completed.

Alexander the Great conquered Persia and Jerusalem about 320 B.C. and Ptolemy I ruled after that until 198 B.C. The Seleucids attempted to make it a Greek center, but this effort came to ruin because of Judas Maccabees and his brother's revolt against them (see I & II Maccabees).

Rome ruled next and set Herod the Great over Israel about 38 B.C. and he ruled for about 40 years. Herod rebuilt and modernized Jerusalem and constructed many fine structures around Israel.

His greatest work was the rebuilding of the temple. Part of the walls that Herod built around the Temple Mount still remain in existence today. Some of the stones in the retaining walls around the Temple Mount weigh 100 tons each. We might conjecture that God permitted Herod's building because he was getting Jerusalem and Israel ready for Jesus, King of Kings and Lord of Lords.

Jerusalem has been an important city since not long after the Tower of Babel. Noah's Flood ended about 2348 B.C.; the Tower of Babel came about 2248 B.C. and Jerusalem was founded about 2000 B.C. (As previously stated, early dating of this period is somewhat arbitrary and open to discussion. These dates could be adjusted backward several hundred years, probably not forward.)

THE GIHON SPRING

The word Gihon in Hebrew means gushing or pulsating. The flow of water from the Gihon spring still increases and decreases. The name is still appropriate. Water in Israel has always been necessary for the existence of a city. The Gihon produces a large quantity of water, more than the city normally required in its early days. It was not only used for the city's needs, but the excess was used to irrigate crops down the valley.

KING DAVID AND THE GIHON

A second reason that Jerusalem was chosen as a place to build a city was that it was on steep hills. With its walls it became an easily-defended fortress.

As already said, when David wanted to capture Jerusalem from the Jebusites, they said the "blind and the lame could defend Jerusalem against David." David said he and his men would reach the blind and lame through the water shaft, which they did. This must have been a daunting task, climbing 55 feet straight up through a large hole.

This shaft had its beginning at the Gihon spring.

THE WARREN SHAFT AT THE GIHON

Charles Warren, while excavating, discovered the shaft to the Gihon spring from inside the walls of Jerusalem in 1860. It bears his name today. There is a tunnel that goes from the Jebusite city down through the rock to a vertical shaft that drops 55 feet to intercept a horizontal tunnel from the Gihon spring to the base of Warren's Shaft. This was so water could be drawn inside the city walls to supply their needs.

The Jebusites had tunneled down about 50 feet through the solid rock to a well that dropped another 55 feet to the water below. This shaft is still used to walk from the surface down an incline to the vertical shaft that dropped 55 feet to the water. After entering the cave from the spring side and going a few feet into a tunnel, one can look up through this large hole where water was drawn from the spring to the city above.

From the top a person could walk down a tunnel on a flight of stairs to a pool holding water drawn from the well. Or they could walk farther down the stairs and draw water from the well itself. This made it possible for more people to access water than if all had to draw water bucket by bucket up 55 feet.

Hezekiah later cut a shaft through the rock from the Gihon spring to a pool called the Pool of Siloam. Its purpose was two-fold, first to make getting water easier for the people and second to serve as a holding tank for times when heavy use of the water was more than the spring could supply. The water would continue to run during low use times and this kept the pool filled with water for high use times.

Today a person can enter from the Jebusite tunnel above and through Warren's Shaft down the stairs to the holding pool and on down stairs to the well and on through a modern shaft to the Gihon Spring itself. The last set of stairs was not there in David or Hezekiah's day.

A person can look up this hole from the spring side of the well shaft. It is a mystery how David and his men accomplished an entry through this large well shaft. But enter they did (II Samuel 5:6–10).

KING SOLOMON AT THE GIHON

Solomon was anointed King at the Gihon by Zadok the priest and Nathan the prophet. In that day it must have been an impressive place, certainly it was an important and beautiful location because the city depended on this water for its existence (I Kings 1:32–34).

KING HEZEKIAH AND THE GIHON

As the city grew, getting water up through a 55-foot deep well hole proved a difficult task and most likely was often a very crowded place during the day. By this time city growth meant better use of the water was required. Hezekiah's tunnel and the Siloam pool helped solve this problem.

The Gihon Spring was the only fresh water source in Jerusalem and it was inconvenient and the water was limited in quantity. The spring's volume of water would accommodate only about 2,500 people a day, so a storage place was needed. Therefore Hezekiah dug a tunnel 1,750 feet through the solid rock to provide a more convenient source of water and a place of water storage inside the city walls.

BIBLICAL ARCHAEOLOGY

This water tunnel is said to be one of the two greatest water engineering technology feats of the ancient world, the other one being in Greece.

Why is the tunnel "S" shaped? Various ideas have been suggested as to why it is not straight through, which would have made it 600 feet shorter. The most probable reason is that the engineers followed a natural fissure in the rock, possibly even where water seeped through a crack.

Near the Siloam Pool end of the tunnel there was an inscription inside the tunnel on the wall put there by King Hezekiah. This was cut off of the wall and is now in the British Museum in London. It reads without correction:

> "...when the tunnel was driven through. And this was the way in which it was cut through: While ... were still ... axes, each man toward his fellow, and while there were still three cubits to be cut through, there was heard the voice of a man calling to his fellows, for there was an overlap in the rock on the right and on the left. And when the tunnel was driven through, the quarrymen hewed the rock, each man toward his fellow, axe against axe; and the water flowed from the spring toward the reservoir for 1,200 cubits, and height of the rock above the heads of the quarrymen was 100 cubits."[37]

By these numbers the tunnel would have been 1,800 feet long and there was 150 feet of solid rock above their heads.

---

37 This was written on the stone wall near where the water shaft entered the Pool of Siloam. This was cut out of the rock and now is in the British Museum in London. The author has seen the site from which the writing was taken as well as the actual writing in the British Museum.

DR. CHARLES CRANE

THE GARDEN OF GETHSEMANE

Just across the Kidron Valley from the Temple Mount is the Garden of Gethsemane. Here it was that Jesus and His Apostles prayed and where the soldiers came to arrest Jesus.

Imagine the soldiers coming in the night with torches burning to light their way, down from the Fortress of Antonia on the Temple Mount, out the eastern gate, down through the Kidron Valley, and across to where Jesus was praying. Certainly He knew they were coming and He could have seen them coming. If He had wished, he could have easily escaped, but He did not.

There He prayed under the old olive trees. Some of these olive trees are still there and are over 2,700 years old. They were mature trees when Jesus was there. We can retrace His steps throughout this night of shame. Jesus was taken from here to the High Priest Caiaphas' house. We will come back to that a bit later.

THE COURTYARD OF THE PRAETORIUM GUARD

At the northwest corner of the Temple Mount were the four towers of the Roman Garrison. In the western part of the fortress was a courtyard where soldiers could muster and await their next assignment. It was in this area that the soldiers played with Jesus while he was awaiting trial. There they mocked him and placed the purple robe and crown of thorns on him.

Jerusalem is also a tel, as has already been stated, with several cities having been built on top of the previous one. In a church building, next to the Roman fortress, they were having problems with a water leak underneath their building. In hunting the source of this leak they dug down some 30–40 feet. They were surprised by what they found. There was the courtyard of the Praetorium Guard, with the roadway in and out of the Roman garrison.

Those looking for the source of the water leak found a large area of pavement with games cut into the paving stones. One game they found cut into the pavement is somewhat like what we call Chinese checkers today. This is the very place where the soldiers had tormented Jesus. It is a reminder that the Bible is a record of actual events and places.

THE HIGH PRIEST'S HOUSE AND DUNGEON

During this night when shame was heaped upon Jesus he was taken to the High Priest Caiaphas' house (Luke 22:54) after leaving the Garden of Gethsemane. This very house has been found by archaeologists. The stairway up to the house, on which Jesus was led, has been unearthed.

After an examination by the High Priest and scribes they abused Jesus, spitting upon Him, slugging Him in the face and slapping Him (Matthew 27:57–68). Then He was put in the dungeon in the basement of the house. This very basement and dungeon have been found. David prophesied what they would do to Jesus at this time in Psalm 88. Jesus was abused and thrown into the pit. The Bible is a real record of real events.

> For my soul is full of troubles, and my life draws near to Sheol. I am counted among those who go down to the pit; I am a man who has no strength, like one set loose among the dead, like the slain that live in the grave, like those whom you remember no more, for they are cut off from your hand. You have put me in the depths of the pit, in the regions dark and deep. Your wrath lies heavy upon me, and you overwhelm me with all your waves. You have caused my companions to shun me; you have made me

a horror to them. I am shut in so that I cannot escape; my eye grows dim through sorrow ... O LORD, why do you cast my soul away? ... Your wrath has swept over me ... You have caused my beloved and my friend to shun me; my companions have become darkness (Psalm 88:3-18).

These things did not happen to David, but did to Jesus, and it is now possible to go to the very place where they happened. In the basement there was a dungeon with a round hole in the ceiling; the only way in or out was through this hole. The prisoner was dropped into the pit, dropping 10–12 feet into this awful place. Jesus suffered here all alone even his beloved friend John had deserted him.

CALVARY AND THE GARDEN TOMB

The exact location of Mt. Calvary and the Tomb of Jesus are not absolutely known. Helena, mother of Emperor Constantine, came to Israel in the fourth century A.D. and tried to locate where the biblical events took place. She claimed to have prayed and she said God showed her where these events happened. The place she identified as Christ's tomb is now the Catholic Church site. It seems to bear little resemblance to the events described in the Bible.

The British General Gordon was stationed in Jerusalem. He was interested to know where Jesus's tomb actually was. He did not believe that the Catholic site was correct. While stationed there he spent his extra time trying to find the correct place.

The Gospels gave him several clues about where Jesus was crucified and buried. It says it was outside the city walls; it was a place called "the Skull"; it was where many people passed by; He was buried in a new tomb, in a garden nearby, and the tomb was hewn from solid rock, so a stone could be rolled in front of the entrance and so on. Using these clues, General Gordon searched to find such a place.

The author remembers his first trip there in 1972. The guide was a retired Englishman, and with a charming accent he showed us Gordon's Calvary and tomb.

We began by looking at the cliff with the eye sockets and nose of a skull in the solid rock. He led us a few yards away to a gigantic cistern that would hold hundreds of thousands of gallons of water. To have a garden there would have required a cistern that would hold lots of water, as there was no fresh water system to irrigate the garden. He showed us an ancient winepress that had been unearthed by the archaeologists. Then he led us to a tomb cut out of the solid rock, with a trench in front where a stone could be rolled in front of the opening. He told us that the large stone was still there when General Gordon first found the place.

The tomb had later been turned into a church, with Christian symbols cut into the rock. The tomb was examined to find out if anyone had actually been buried there and decomposed. The results were negative, showing no signs that anyone had ever decomposed there. General Gordon asked himself why this grave had been made into a church, with crosses and religious symbols. He wondered why such a tomb had never been used. This information convinced him he had found Jesus' tomb.

Our guide said, "Am I going to tell you for certain that this is Jesus' empty tomb?" He said, "I cannot do that, but if this is not the place it was a place just like this, for this place matches all of the biblical information and is the only place that does so."

Yes, Jesus was crucified at the place of the skull, where people would be walking by, outside the gates of the city, where there was a garden nearby, in which Joseph of Arimathea's tomb was. The tomb had a large stone that rolled across the opening; Peter ran up, stooped down, and looked in. Gordon's Calvary and tomb and biblical information match.

ABRAHAM AND MELCHIZEDEK

Genesis 14:17–20 says:

> After his return from the defeat of Chedorlaomer and the kings ... Melchizedek went out to meet him at the Valley of Shaveh (that is, the King's Valley). And Melchizedek king of Salem (That is Jerusalem) brought out bread and wine. (He was priest of God Most High.) And he blessed him and said. "Blessed be Abram by God Most High. Possessor of heaven and earth; and blessed be God Most High. Who has delivered your enemies into your hand!" And Abram gave him a tenth of everything.

The valley of Shaveh is one and the same as the Kidron Valley, the one that runs between Calvary, the Temple Mount, and the Garden of Gethsemane. Here the type of Christ (Melchizedek) and the type of the Christian (Abraham) broke bread, drank the wine, and Abraham gave an offering. It is just like our church services today. It is a prophecy of the time to come when the King comes to His valley in the Triumphal Entry into Jerusalem through the King's Valley; the King comes to Gethsemane to pray; the King is taken to the High Priest's house across the valley; and He, the King, is abused at the Praetorium courtyard. It is where Calvary and the King's tomb was, and the place where the King's resurrection took place. Certainly it is "the King of Kings Valley."

Where was this? It was where Melchizedek and Abraham sat and had communion and Abraham, the type of the

Christian, gave Melchizedek, the type of Christ, his tithe. But more than that, this valley was where the central events of all of history took place when the King Jesus came there to the Praetorium, Gethsemane, Caiaphas' house, Golgotha, and His tomb. It is the "King's Valley" or valley of the King of Kings, the Lord Jesus Christ. We have now visited the city of the Great King, Jesus our Lord. Zion is the city of the Great King.

THE CROSS WAS HIS OWN

They borrowed a bed to lay His head,
When Christ the Lord came down,
They borrowed the ass in the mountain pass:
For Him to ride to town:
But the crown that He wore,
And the cross He bore were His own—
The cross was His own.

He borrowed the bread when the crowd He fed,
On the grassy mountain side,
He borrowed the dish of broken fish,
With which He satisfied:
But the crown that He wore,
And the cross that He bore, were his own—
The cross was His own.

He borrowed the ship in which to sit,
To teach the multitude.
He borrowed a nest in which to rest,
He had never a home so rude:
But the crown that He wore,
And the cross that He bore, were His own—
The cross was His own.

> He borrowed a room on His way to the tomb
> The passion lamb to eat,
> They borrowed a cave for Him a grave,
> They borrowed a winding sheet:
> But the crown that He wore,
> And the cross that He bore, were His own—
> The cross was His own.

Author unknown

The Bible is the written word, through which we know the Living Word, Jesus. The Bible is a unit from one end to the other, an inspired book, the truth; it need not be proven, that has already happened years ago. But isn't it wonderful to be able to visit the exact sites where the biblical events have transpired? We are following the families of man from the flood of Noah and on into the future.

Chapter Fifteen

Ninevah and Babylon

An effort has been made to follow chronologically the archaeological discoveries from the flood of Noah until the time of Christ. In the last chapter we looked at some of the discoveries that are in and around Jerusalem, beginning with father Abraham and on to the time of Christ. In this chapter we will be looking at the two captivities of Israel and then 150 years later the captivity of Judah. This fits in the middle of our Jerusalem study.

Our interest in Nineveh and Babylon relate to their often being mentioned in the Bible and that they were the two nations that were used to punish a rebellious Israel, first in the dispersion of the ten northern tribes (Israel), and then in the captivity and return of the two southern tribes (Judah).

Both cities have ancient origins that are told about in the Bible in Genesis 10:8–11.

> Cush fathered Nimrod; he was the first on earth to be a mighty man. He was a mighty hunter before the Lord. Therefore it is said "Like Nimrod a mighty hunter before the Lord." The beginning of his kingdom was Babel, Erech, Accad and Calneh, in the land of Shinar. From that land he went into Assyria and built Nineveh, …

NINEVEH

Nineveh was one of the first cities to become the headquarters of a world power. It was the city the Prophet Jonah was sent to evangelize.

> Now the word of the LORD came to Jonah the son of Amittai, saying, arise, go to Nineveh, that great city and call out against it, for their evil has come up before me (Jonah 1:1—4:11).

We remember the Bible account that tells how Jonah was sent east to Nineveh but instead headed west to flee from this task. His actions are understandable since Nineveh was Israel's mortal enemy. He ended up taking a submarine ride in a great fish God had prepared to swallow him. The fish couldn't keep a backslidden prophet on his stomach and spit him out on the ground. Jonah got the message and headed to Nineveh as God had commanded.

Nineveh is described in the book of Jonah as being a great city, three days' journey across (Jonah 3:3). This most certainly describes the Nineveh area, likely not all within the walls, but also the population outside the walls. Nineveh was at that time the largest city the world had ever had, with a population estimated at least 150,000 people, probably more.

Jonah's preaching was successful and the people repented in sack cloth and fasting, from the greatest to the least of the population. God did not destroy the city as Jonah had hoped and Jonah was angry that God did not destroy them.

NINEVEH'S ORIGIN AND HISTORY

Let us take a closer look at Nineveh, its origin and history. Nineveh was in upper Mesopotamia; today this is northern

BIBLICAL ARCHAEOLOGY

Iraq, on the eastern bank of the Tigris River and it was the capital of the Assyrian Empire. It was the largest city in the world for a period of about 50 years.

Its demise was started by a bitter civil war that broke out and the city ended up being sacked. The Babylonians, Medes, Persians, Chaldeans, and Cimmerians took it in 612 B.C. Today its ruins lie across the river from the modern city of Mosul.

The ancient city, founded by Nimrod, has been said by some to have been founded 6000 B.C. Of course we know that this is fallacious. No pre-flood city has been found and this would have meant that Nineveh, if that old, was in existence long before the flood. There is no archaeological evidence to suggest that this could be true.

Sennacherib made it a grand city about 700 B.C. with new streets, squares, and glorious palaces which were the finest in the world.

Excavations have identified his palace as being 1,650 feet by 794 feet. It had 80 rooms and was lined with sculptures and art work. The foundations were of limestone and brick. The walls were 72 feet high. Many cuneiform tablets have been found within. It is estimated that there were 160 million bricks in his palace.

Sennacherib's city was 1,730 acres within the walls and as already stated, at least 150,000 inhabitants. (Remember that Jericho was about 14 acres and Megiddo about 100.) Aqueducts carried water into the city from forty miles away. There were twice as many people in Nineveh as in Babylon at that time. But the peace and greatness of Nineveh was short lived. It lasted only until 627 B.C. when internal civil war began and weakened it. It was attacked in 616 and lost its independence.

It seems Nineveh grew to greatness for the purpose of punishing Israel for their sinfulness and idolatry, at least this was one of its accomplishments. The ten northern tribes were captured and dispersed among the Assyrians to be lost to history. Thus we call them the "Ten Lost Tribes." Efforts to identify them as a distinct people today have failed. Efforts to teach that England and America are descendants of the ten lost tribes have failed miserably. They intermarried with the Assyrians and other peoples, and faded completely from history.

Assyria's and Nineveh's claim to fame is that Sennacherib came to Israel and captured all their fortified cities, taking the ten northern tribes away to Assyria. This brought about the end of the northern Kingdom that had been established after Solomon's death by Jeroboam. This brought an end to ten of the twelve tribes, leaving only Judah, Benjamin, and some of the tribe of Levi.

When Sennacherib came to take Jerusalem, with his General Rabshakeh, he found a much more difficult task than with the other cities of Israel. Most important was that the Prophets had been listened to more carefully by Judah. King Hezekiah was a fine king, possibly the best of all of the kings of Israel and Judah.

When Rabshakeh cursed and threatened Judah and Jerusalem, Hezekiah turned to prayer and he covered himself with sackcloth. God heard his prayers and Sennacherib awakened one morning to find 180,000 dead soldiers. He went home to be killed by his own sons in their Pagan temple. Read Isaiah 36 and 37 and compare II Kings 18:13ff.

ARCHAEOLOGY OF NINEVEH

What has been found of importance at Nineveh? So completely had Nineveh disappeared from the map that some unbelieving scholars questioned what the Bible and other ancient histories had to say about its existence, claiming that it was only a mythical city.

In 1820 Claudius James Rich spent four months sketching the mounds across the river from Mosul, which he suspected were Nineveh. In 1845 Layard definitely identified the site as Nineveh and uncovered the ruins of the magnificent palaces of the Assyrian kings that have now become widely known. Thousands of inscriptions have been found.

The principal mound is called Koyunjik and it covers about 100 acres and it rises above the plain an average of 90 feet. It contains the palaces of Sennacherib and Assurbanipal. Sennacherib was the king who captured the ten tribes and raided Judah. His is the grandest palace of all. This palace was the size of three city blocks. Layard found it in 1849–50.

The prize find was found in the palace of Sennacherib, by Layard, Rassam, and Rawlinson in 1852–54. It was Sennacherib's library, originally holding 100,000 volumes. About one-third have been recovered, and these tablets are in the British Museum in London. He had his scribes research and then copy the libraries of ancient Babylon and many of the histories before his time for his own library. The result was he had preserved ancient Babylonian literature.

The find of this great library does not compare with the find at Ebla, since Ebla is so much earlier and confirms so much of the early Old Testament.

BABYLON

According to the Bible, Babylon was founded by the great man Nimrod. Both Nineveh and Babylon were built alongside the rivers flowing from the snows of Mt. Ararat. After Noah's Ark landed there, the survivors naturally looked for good places to settle. The Tigris and Euphrates supplied plenty of water and the climate was warm and inviting. Food was easily raised and civilization prospered.

God had clearly told them, "Be fruitful and multiply and fill the earth" Genesis 9:1, and again, "And you, be fruitful and multiply, increase greatly on the earth and multiply in it" (Genesis 9:7).

But what did the people do? "Then they said, 'Come, let us build ourselves a city and a tower with its top in the heavens, and let us make a name for ourselves, lest we be dispersed over the face of the whole earth'" (Genesis 11:4). The result of their rebellion was that God confounded their speech and they were forced to disperse. Therefore the place was called "Babel, because there the Lord confused the language of all the earth. And from there the Lord dispersed them over the face of all the earth" (Genesis 11:8–9).

The meaning of Babylon, then, is babbling, confusion, or confounded, because God gave them many different languages. We have already discussed the Tower of Babel and will not say more here. But let us look at the geography and history of Babylon.

GEOGRAPHY AND HISTORY OF BABYLON

The ancient city ruins are about 53 miles south of modern Baghdad. The city was founded about 2286 by Nimrod (Belus is possibly the same person). It became an important city, and for over 1,000 years played an important role in world history.

Babylon was the scene of Daniel's remarkable ministry. It was the wonder city of the ancient world. It was situated in the cradle of the human race, possibly near the Garden of Eden,

BIBLICAL ARCHAEOLOGY

and not too far from where Noah's Ark rested on Mt. Ararat. It was where the Tower of Babel was built and the place from which God dispersed the nations.

Babylon was at the zenith of its power during the reign of Nebuchadnezzar and of the Prophet Daniel. These were the glory days of Babylon. Nebuchadnezzar, who was Daniel's friend, never tired of building and beautifying Babylon during his 45-year reign.

One ancient historian (most certainly an exaggeration), said that it was 60 miles around the walls with 15 miles on each side. The walls were 300 feet high and 80 feet thick, extending 35 feet below the ground surface. He said there were 250 towers on the walls and that two, two-horse chariots could travel side by side on top of the walls. That there were also wide moats around the walls, 100 gates of brass, a tunnel under the river 15 feet wide and 12 feet high, as the city was built on both sides of the Euphrates River, with ferries and one large bridge thirty feet wide across the river. This account is probably not accurate as archaeology has found a large city but smaller than described above. The city had a population estimated of more than 200,000. It was still a massive and impressive city.[38]

Nebuchadnezzar's Palace, into which Daniel would have often gone, was one of the most magnificent buildings ever erected on earth. It was uncovered in 1899–1912 by the archaeologist Robert Koldewey.

At his palace were the Hanging Gardens which were one of the Seven Wonders of the ancient world, built by Nebuchadnezzar for his Median Queen, the beautiful daughter of Cyaxeres.

---

38 *Halley's Handbook*, page 300.

Cyaxeres had helped Nebuchadnezzar's father conquer Nineveh. The gardens were built on several tiers of arches, one on top of the other, which made several platforms 400 feet square on top of these terraces. The top of each terrace was covered with gardens of flowers, shrubs, and trees. These gardens were watered from a reservoir at the top filled with water from the river, raised by hydraulic pumps. Under the arches were luxurious apartments. These were the grounds of the Palace. The ruins of the hanging gardens have been found.

NEBUCHADNEZZAR CAPTURES JUDAH WITH DANIEL

Nebuchadnezzar captured Jerusalem and took them away into captivity. There was not a lot of bloodshed since the king surrendered and the people were deported to Babylon. The Temple was looted and destroyed. Read about this in II Kings 24 & 25. What happened to the Ark of the Covenant? This question remains and probably never will be answered.

This led to the terrible exodus from Israel to Babylon. Those who had lived in luxury were forced to walk the hundreds of miles across the burning desert, seeing their families and children suffer. Many would have died along the way.

The book of Daniel gives a picture of what happened to the people who made it to Babylon. Many were skilled craftsmen, and the younger and brightest were trained to serve the nation. This account is found in Daniel 1:1 & 5; 2:1.

The book of Esther (About 474 B.C.) tells about efforts to wipe out the Jews and how Esther helped save the Jewish people from annihilation when Haman plotted to wipe out the Jews throughout the Empire (see Esther chapter 3). She became the Queen through the providence of God and skill of her uncle Mordecai.

In all of these events God was preserving the seed of Abraham and David and helping to prepare the way to fulfil His promises to them that in their seed the whole world would be blessed. Assyria and Babylon were a part of God's working out the process of salvation that we enjoy today.

BABLYON'S EARLIER HISTORY

Now back to a much earlier time when Hammurabi (Probably Amraphel of Genesis 14:1) helped build Babylon into a great city and conquered the surrounding area to enlarge his kingdom. He has been made famous, not for making a great kingdom but because of his law code that he had inscribed on pillars and placed at the entrances of the cities he ruled. Hammurabi did not rule the world but was the head of an important city state.

About 1595 B.C. the Hittites, from Asia Minor (modern Turkey), took over Babylon and also extended their rule as far away as Egypt. They can probably be identified as the Hyksos Kings that ruled Egypt through the period when the Patriarch Joseph came to a second position in Egypt.

The Assyrians (Nineveh) ruled Babylon from 911–609 B.C. Nabapolassar, of Babylon, threw off this Assyrian rule. Nebuchadnezzar followed and ruled from 609–564 B.C., 45 years. He completely rebuilt the city into the most glorious city on earth. As has been said, his palace and its hanging gardens were considered to be one of the seven wonders of the ancient world.

Nebuchadnezzar most likely came to power to be a messenger from God to punish Judah for her rebellion and disobedience against Him. They had neglected their Sabbaths, their tithes, their sabbatical years and years of jubilee. His laws had been profaned and they had turned to idolatry. God wanted, once and for all, to cure them of their sin and idolatry and preserve Judah to make way for Jesus.

It is a reminder that the law of God is always the same; people either give God what is His or the devourer takes it. It is still true today. Disobey or rob God and it will always lead to devastation and trouble.

During their time in exile God raised up from among them people like Daniel and Esther, to help preserve and direct Judah so that after they had learned their lessons they could return to Israel and rebuild it. Ezra and Nehemiah, and others, led in this rebuilding work. This made it possible for the final preparations to be made for the coming of the Messiah.

In 539, Cyrus the Great conquered Babylon and his job was to make it possible for the Jews to return to their homeland and to rebuild the temple in Jerusalem (see II Chronicles 36).

Babylon's eventual destruction was predicted by the Prophets.

> Behold, I am stirring up the Medes against them, ... And Babylon, the glory of kingdoms, the splendor and pomp of the Chaldeans, will be like Sodom and Gomorrah when God overthrew them. It will never be inhabited or lived in for all generations; no Arab will pitch his tent there; no shepherds will make their flocks lie down there. But wild animals will lie down there, and their houses will be full of howling creatures; ... (Isaiah 13:17–21).

> ... and Babylon shall become a heap of ruins, the haunt of jackals, a horror and a hissing, without inhabitants ... How Babylon is taken, the praise of the whole earth seized! How Babylon has become a horror among the nations! ... Therefore, behold, the days are coming when I will punish the images of Babylon: her whole land shall be put

to shame and all her slain shall fall in the midst of her ... (Jeremiah 51:37–47).

Saddam Hussein was in the process of trying to rebuild Babylon when he was killed. To the best of the author's knowledge this building project now lies unfinished, covered with sand, and is returning to the desert and still a place for wild animals and owls.

ARCHAEOLOGY OF BABYLON

Here is a brief list of those who have done archaeological work at Babylon:

1. Claudius James Rich, 1811–12 and 1817. He led the first exploration, but in fact did very little.

2. Austen Henry Layard made a brief visit in 1850.

3. Henry Rawlinson and George Smith made another brief visit in 1854 and again from 1879–1882 which led to widespread looting.

4. The first real scientific exploration was done by Robert Holdeway, 1899–1917.

The present day ruins are mounds and remains of the city and its great buildings. They are mostly on the east side of the river and cover an area about 3½ by 3 miles. There are three principal mounds, the largest of which is 130 feet high. Another mound is 70 feet high and covers the area where the Palace and Hanging Garden were.

Where the Tower of Babel once stood is a large hole in the ground, since the high-quality fired bricks have been mined by surrounding area residents for their building projects.

Nothing remains of it, even to the bottom of its foundation, deep in a hole.

Here again we have learned that if the Bible tells about events and places they really happened and the places most often can be found. Two of the world's great kingdoms, Assyria and Babylonia, with their capital cities, Nineveh and Babylon, have been found. We even know where the people's houses were that are mentioned in the Bible.

> All scripture is breathed out by God and profitable for teaching, for reproof, for correction, and for training in righteousness, that the man of God may be complete, equipped for every good work (II Timothy 3:16–17).

Jesus said; "... the Scripture cannot be broken" (John 10:35).

> Suggested Reading and sources:
> *Everyday Life in Bible Times*, National Geographic Society
> Cornfield, Gaalyah and Freedman, David Noel,
> *Archaeology of the Bible Book by Book*.
> *Halley's Handbook*
> Kenyon, Kathleen M., *The Bible and Recent Archaeology*.
> The Internet.

Chapter Sixteen

Bible Origins and the Dead Sea Scrolls

Our study has shown that writing was highly developed immediately after Noah and his family exited the Ark. There is lots of evidence to support this fact. This seems adequate proof that Noah and his family were not only literate, but highly literate. Building the Ark could not have been accomplished unless Noah was brilliant and skilled.

The 17,000 clay tablets found at Ebla in Syria have been dated 2240 B.C., which was not long after Noah and his family came from the Ark. Among these tablets there are references made about the Royal Library at Ebla, which has not yet been found.

This proves that writing was already widespread. It is safe to conclude that writing had to have been well developed long before the flood and that Noah and his family almost certainly carried written documents with them onto the ark. For Noah to have constructed the Ark he would have to have been literate.

In chapter thirteen we learned about many different ancient written documents, proving that ancient people had highly developed writing skills and languages. We gave examples of more than twenty ancient writings, in various languages. We talked about the Rosetta Stone and the Behistun Rock, which helped us decipher languages that had long been unreadable.

The Law Code of Hammurabi and the huge libraries at Nineveh and Babylon gave additional proof of the highly developed languages and people's writing skills back into the dim past. Egypt had their own language that was different from the other nations; it too was highly developed.

Among all these writings, not one tablet or inscription has been found that dates before the flood of Noah. There are only post-flood writings. This suggests that everything that was not on the Ark, was destroyed. Yet Noah and his family came off of the Ark with highly developed writing skills.

It is reasonable to conclude that Noah and his family all spoke the same language. How then is it that there are so many different families of languages on the earth not long after the flood? This poses a difficult problem for people who do not accept the biblical account. This problem can best be explained by the biblical history of the Tower of Babel and the confusion of the languages of people and their dispersion over the earth.

With the confusion of languages, those who could talk to each other naturally gathered in different nations. But the main point to be established is that writing was well developed by the time of Job and long before Moses wrote the Pentateuch. To suggest that the Bible could not have been written when it claims to have been is nonsense.

THE BIBLE BOOKS AND WRITERS

It is almost certain that Job is the oldest book in our Bibles. The evidence for the ancient nature of Job is that it takes place in a period sometimes called "The Patriarchal Age." This was the period before Moses when the father of the family was the priest before God and organized religion was not yet developed.

BIBLICAL ARCHAEOLOGY

The book of Job shows no knowledge of the writings of Moses, as do all the other Old Testament books. It would have been natural to refer to the Law of Moses if it had been in existence when the book of Job was written.

Therefore, dating Job in the 16th Century B.C. makes sense. It must have been written early, but after the flood, because Job was from the land of Uz. Where was that? We do not know for sure.

Uz was a direct descendant of Noah's son Shem and his son Aram. This means he was a godly man of Semitic descent (Genesis 10:21–23). This would suggest a Mesopotamian or Canaanite location. If not in Canaan it was likely not far from there. Job would then have been written some time after the Tower of Babel and among those who spoke the Hebrew language. This helps us know that Job is the oldest Bible book.

The five books of Moses, called the Pentateuch, were written about 1491 B.C. Writing was highly developed at that time and had been for hundreds of years. Moses had been educated in Egypt, the most advanced nation on earth at that time. This means he was well qualified to record the Books of the Law.

The other Old Testament books fit chronologically in sequence alongside the period in which they fit into Israel's history. They follow the history of Israel from Joshua, and all the writers in-between, to the latter Prophets: Daniel (540); Zechariah (520-480 B.C.); Ezra and Nehemiah (538 B.C.); Haggai (460 B.C.); and Malachi (450 B.C.). This led to a period that is called the silent years, when for a period of 400 years no prophet spoke. This silence was finally broken by the preaching of John the Baptist about A.D. 28 or 29.

The question arises, why did certain books end up being in the Bible, while others did not? What was going on with the

Old Testament books after the death of the last Prophet, and the coming of John the Baptist, and Jesus? Who decided what was Bible and what was not? The answer to these questions is found in the Great Synagogue.

THE GREAT SYNAGOGUE

The Great Synagogue or Assembly came into existence in a period of history about which very little is known, namely the Persian period. According to ancient Jewish tradition and the most ancient writings (like the Talmud), a group of religious leaders, called The Great Synagogue, was formed after the return from captivity. This makes sense because from the time of Moses onward there were leaders of Israel. Moses appointed seventy men (later called the Sanhedrin) who along with the priests were the physical and spiritual leaders of the nation.

After the return to Canaan, Ezra and Nehemiah gathered leaders of Judah together to study and reinstate the Law of Moses. In Nehemiah chapters 8—10 it seems to allude to a select group of men. There is even a list of who these men were. Ezra 2:2 also lists some of these men. Among this group were Ezra, Nehemiah, and Zerubbabel.

While the last of the Prophets were still alive, also including Haggai, Zechariah, and Malachi, a group was formed to lead Judah. This group could have been formed after the example of the 70 men Moses chose to help him lead Israel and that would be called in Jesus' day, the Sanhedrin. This group in Ezra's day was called "The Great Synagogue."

These men, several of which were Prophets of God, placed their stamp of approval on the 33 books of the Old Testament. We have these same books in our Old Testament but divide them into 39 books.

BIBLICAL ARCHAEOLOGY

We call this selection of what was scripture, canonization. (The word "canon" is from a Latin word that means a measure. To canonize is to measure and find that which is measured and meets the standard.) If this group did not do it, then who did? It stands to reason that the Great Synagogue designated which Old Testament books were scripture and which were not. We have already shown there were many other books that could have been chosen.

Later in history there was another person who had a part in the preservation of the unity and purity of the Old Testament. This man was named Simeon the Just. He was probably the High Priest of his time. It is believed he served as head of the Great Synagogue group who passed along the Scripture. They offered continued protection of the scriptures.

By Christ's time there was no confusion on what was or was not Scripture. It had been settled for hundreds of years. Jesus gave his endorsement of the Old Testament books in Luke 24:44. He said that the Law, Psalms, and Prophets spoke of Him. These were the three categories of the Old Testament. Jesus endorsed the 33 Hebrew books and our 39 books. (Remember that the Jews divided the very same books differently than we do.)[39]

THE PRESERVATION OF THE OLD TESTAMENT TEXT

We have said something about scribes already, but more information might be helpful. The scribes were a highly trained, professional group, whose duty was to carefully record and copy important documents. They could be compared to our accountants or lawyers today. They were highly skilled.

---

39 To learn more about this subject, see, *The Bible, the True and Reliable Word of God*, by Charles Crane.

DR. CHARLES CRANE

Among the Jews, the scribes' highest work was the copying of scripture. They had very distinct rules that had to be followed. To us these rules may seem arbitrary, but they assured that the scribe made no mistakes. Here is a brief summary of these rules for copying Scripture:

1. The parchment must be made of the skin of a clean animal.

2. Each column must have no less than 48 or no more than 60 lines.

3. The ink must be of no other color than black and prepared from a special recipe.

4. No word or letter could be written from memory—the scribe must have an authentic and approved manuscript in front of him.

5. He must reverently wipe his pen each time before writing the word for God and must wash his whole body before writing the word Jehovah.

6. Strict rules were given concerning the forms of the letters, spaces between letters, words, and sections, the use of the pen and color of the parchment were prescribed.

7. The revision of a roll must be made within 30 days after the work was finished, otherwise it was worthless. One mistake on a sheet condemned that sheet, and three mistakes on any page condemned the whole manuscript.

8. Every word and every letter were counted, and if a letter was omitted, an extra letter inserted, or if one letter touched another, the manuscript was condemned and was to be destroyed at once.

BIBLICAL ARCHAEOLOGY

It must have been a tedious task to copy scripture. This gives us a brief glimpse of why our scriptures could be handed down over centuries with only a very few small variant readings.

Until the finding of the Dead Sea Scrolls, the oldest known complete Hebrew Bible was the Leningrad Codex (A.D. 1027) which contained the whole Old Testament in Hebrew. (A codex book has leaves in distinction to a scroll that is a roll.) This old Bible is the best representation of the Masoretic text we have and was probably written in Cairo, Egypt, and then taken to Damascus. Today it is at St. Petersburg, Russia. We do have other old Hebrew texts but they are only of parts of the Old Testament and not early. What happened to so many of the old Bibles? They were destroyed by Roman Emperors like Nero and Diocletian, who did their best to wipe out Jewish and Christian faiths.

In A.D. 1947, suddenly the Old Testament scriptures were in the news, due to finding the Dead Sea Scrolls. Among the nearly 15,000 fragments eventually found, there were 380 biblical texts. Some of these removed a time gap of 1,000 years between what we had and what was found. Some of these biblical scrolls, found in the Essenes library, dated as early as the fourth century B.C.

QUMRAN

Where is Qumran located and what was found there? Qumran is a settlement that was near the northwest end of the Dead Sea, not far from Jericho. It is believed that this settlement was inhabited by Essenes. They were one of the three most well-known religious/political parties of Jesus' time. The other two were the Sadducees and Pharisees.

The Essenes were a mystical sect who lived lives of purity, poverty and separation. They organized about 100 B.C. and lasted until the fall of Jerusalem in 72 A.D. Some have conjectured that they may have joined the Zealots that died at Masada. When they saw the destruction coming on Israel by the Romans, they hid their most prized possessions, their libraries, in caves not far from their settlement.

The Essenes may be referred to in such Bible passages as Matthew 18:11–12 and Colossians 2:8, 18 and 23. These verses seem to refer to some of the main ideas fostered by them.

Some have thought that John the Baptist was an Essene, but there is little or no proof for this assertion. He did live a life of asceticism and in the desert, but the similarity stops there.

The Essenes spent a lot of time in Scripture study, Scripture copying, and seeking to live by the Law of Moses. Their most prized possessions must have been their old biblical manuscripts that were in their library. In visiting Qumran one can see the scriptorium, with a convenient place nearby for ritual baths, and a place for their library also close by.

They spoke often of the sons of light and of darkness. They considered themselves to be sons of light and possibly the leaders in Jerusalem to be sons of darkness. The museum in Jerusalem where the Dead Sea Scrolls are kept has this teaching symbolized in the white pottery jar-type lid as the museum's roof and a black wall nearby as representative of sons of darkness.

FINDING THE DEAD SEA SCROLLS

In retrospect, it seems that God must have used the Essenes for the purpose of preserving the Old Testament books as a witness to the accuracy of the Old Testament for us who live in the latter-times.

BIBLICAL ARCHAEOLOGY

A Bedouin shepherd boy was looking for a lost sheep in the Judean wilderness, and as boys are wont to do, he was throwing rocks. He threw a rock into a cave and heard a jar break. Upon further investigation he found many pottery jars with old leather scrolls within. He took some home to their Bedouin tent, thinking the leather might be good for something. They hung them in the tent for some time.

Finding writing on them, and thinking they might be valuable, they were offered for sale to antiquity dealers in the Jerusalem area. When Metropolitan Samuel, of the Syrian Orthodox Christian Church, had the opportunity to buy some of them, he did. Samuel showed them to the visiting American scholar John C. Trevor, who was permitted to take some home to the United States for study. He found that one, the Isaiah scroll, was very old, and determined that it was at least as old as 225 B.C. Other scrolls were even older.

Thus identified, the word spread about how valuable the scrolls were and this led to a massive hunt for others. Eventually, over a nine-year period, about 15,000 scrolls and fragments were found. The scrolls were written mostly in Hebrew. From 1947–1956, eleven caves were found containing scrolls.

At Masada, a scroll burial place was found near the synagogue. According to Jewish law, when a Bible scroll became worn it was to be buried or burned. This was to assure that an old unreadable scroll would not provide a source of error in copying a new scroll. Some of these old worn manuscripts were found there in the scroll graveyard next to the synagogue.

The author had followed, with great interest, the finding of the scrolls. When in Jerusalem in 1972, one of his goals was to meet with Metropolitan Samuel, which he did. Samuel was gracious to receive him and they discussed, for several hours, the history of the scrolls. Samuel still had some of the jars in which the scrolls were stored and some fragments that he let the author inspect. Samuel had firsthand knowledge of what had been so widely publicized in books and the news. He told the author about buying them, his meetings with Dr. Trevor, and what was eventually found.

Initially it was reported that 330 of the original 900 scrolls were biblical. This number has now grown, due to additional finds, to 380 or more biblical scrolls. The initial report was that every Old Testament book but Esther was found. Later it was reported that Nehemiah had not been found. This is probably because, very early, Ezra and Nehemiah were put together as one book.

Not only was every book but Esther found, but multiple copies of many of the books turned up. Of course many were fragmentary, but gave witness to the accuracy of our more recent copies.

Dating the various Bible books has continued. Isaiah was at first dated to 225 B.C. and that date has now been moved backward to 351 B.C. One property deed has been dated at 408 B.C. Most of the biblical portion of the scrolls date well before the birth of Christ.

THE VALUE OF THE SCROLLS

The scrolls help us know that our Old Testament scriptures have come down to us remarkably unchanged. We now have evidence that takes us back well over 1,000 years before what we had in 1950. Dr. John Trevor said that the kinds of changes between Hebrew Bible text we use today and the variations of reading them, and the ancient Isaiah scroll, were so minute as to be of interest only to biblical scholars.

BIBLICAL ARCHAEOLOGY

The words of Jesus have been confirmed: "For truly I say to you, until heaven and earth pass away, not an iota, not a dot, will pass from the Law until all is accomplished" (Matthew 5:18).

The value of the Dead Sea Scrolls cannot be measured in dollars; as for the value to believers, it is beyond any earthly measure. We have had confirmed to us, in modern time, that our Bible has been carefully preserved for us today.

Qumran, with its library hidden in the caves, is probably the most significant archaeological find from the pre-Christian era. Certainly with reference to our Bible text, it tops the list of Old Testament written finds. We are supremely blessed by knowing God's word has come down to us without a shadow of doubt as to its accuracy.

Suggested Reading:
Crane, Charles A., *The Bible the True and Reliable Word of God*.
Trevor, John C. Any of his writings about the Dead Scrolls is valuable reading.

Chapter Seventeen

Herod the Great—The Builder

Matthew 24:1–22 – "The Olivet Discourse"

In what is called The Olivet Discourse, Jesus is asked three questions by His Apostles that He answers. These questions relate to the destruction of Jerusalem, a time of terrible trouble that was coming soon, and finally the end of the age. Jesus makes it plain that in Matthew 24:4–34 he is speaking of things that will happen in the lifetime of the Apostles. In verse thirty-four He says; "Truly, I say to you, this generation will not pass away until all these things take place." Jesus' message is clear that a terrible time of trouble, such as the world has never seen, nor will see, is coming. In this chapter we will examine the archaeological discoveries that support Jesus' words.

HEROD THE GREAT

Herod was called "The Great" to distinguish him from his sons who ruled after him, also called Herod. Basically Herod was an evil man. But in some ways he was great, particularly in his great building projects; the remains of many of these survive to this day. They paint a picture of the grandeur he brought to Israel in preparation for Israel's true glory days, when the King of Kings would come to Israel and Jerusalem.

BIBLICAL ARCHAEOLOGY

Herod was born about 74 B.C. in Idumea which is south of Judah. He was the second son of Antipater, a high ranking official under Hyrcanus. Herod's father was an Edomite whose family had converted to Judaism, whether voluntarily or under compulsion remains open to discussion.

His history is lengthy and for our purpose here we will only take a brief overview. He was first appointed governor of Galilee when he was about 26 years old. He had the backing of Rome, but was not accepted by the Jewish Sanhedrin because of his brutality and lineage.

Jerusalem had come under Roman control about 63 B.C. but the Parthians (Greeks) took temporary control of Jerusalem and Herod had to flee to Rome in fear of his life. There he was unexpectedly appointed King of the Jews by the Roman Senate about 39 B.C.

He was already married to Doris with whom he had a son. Upon his return to Israel he took a second wife, Mariamne. He may have loved her, but the marriage was primarily political.

He became sole ruler of Israel by edict of the Roman Senate in 37 B.C. Although he claimed to be a Jew he was not accepted as such by the Jewish people. There was probably more than one reason for this rejection. His behavior was brutal and not what would be expected of a godly man. Also, according to Jewish law it took seven generations for one to be considered a full-fledged Jew after conversion to Judaism. Until that time had passed, a person was considered a proselyte of the gate.

He had 2,000 bodyguards who accompanied him, some of the brightest and strongest men in Israel. He used them to brutally remove anyone who resisted his rule. Thus he quickly consolidated his reign and power.

Flavius Josephus' (also known as Joseph Mathaius) early writings represent Herod in a more positive light than his later writings do. His evil works overshadowed his good deeds.

His claim to fame was his lavish building projects. He rebuilt the Temple mount and Temple. He redesigned and modernized Jerusalem to a level it had never seen before. His projects included Caesarea by the Sea, Hebron, the Herodian, Masada, Macharaeus, Gamla, and many other great building projects. Some of these projects were almost super-human in achievement.

Herod was always paranoid but more so as he aged. Much of his building was to provide security for himself and those who supported him. He killed people of whom he was suspicious, even those he loved most, including a son, and his favorite wife.

His most dastardly act was the massacre of the innocents at the birth of Christ in Bethlehem. Jesus' birth made quite a stir, with the visitation of the angels, shepherds, and wise men from the east. This was reported to Herod and he feared the report of the birth of a child who was to be the King of the Jews.

Herod ruled from 37 B.C. to 4 B.C. according to history. This for some has become a cause to question the biblical accounts of the birth of Jesus and Herod's killing of the children. This problem is solved by learning that the Romans made a mistake with our calendar; Jesus was born 4–5 B.C., and our calendars are behind 4–5 years.

Herod's death is described by many different historians, like Josephus, and in modern times by the biographical historian James Michener in his book *The Source*.

According to Josephus, he ordered that the leading citizen of every city was to be killed at his death. This was to assure that

Israel would truly mourn his passing. Of course when he was dead this order was not carried out.

His last years were miserable and he spent a lot of time in Jericho, where there were hot spring pools that would ease his misery. He possibly suffered from some sort of STD that ate away his body and filled his days with agony.

When he finally died, he had prepared a burial spot at the Herodium near Jerusalem. According to Michener's history, the funeral procession was still leaving Jericho when the first of it was arriving at the Herodium.

The author had a life-long friend, Zac Jamjoum, who was born and raised in Jerusalem. His family has owned the same house there for more than 400 years. He and the author shared several interests, including coin collecting and collecting ancient archaeological artifacts. He made it possible for the author to obtain old biblical coins and his most prized artifact, a Herodian lamp from the excavation of Herod's palace at the Herodium.

HEROD THE GREAT'S BUILDING PROJECTS

THE HERODIUM

We will briefly look at four of Herod's massive building projects. Each was a part of his security system for Israel. This was in part due to his personal paranoia but also for the government's safety. One of the purposes of these fortresses was a gigantic early warning system.

The Herodium is a cone-shaped hill about seven-and-one-half miles south of Jerusalem and three miles from Bethlehem. The hill is the highest peak in the Judean desert at 2,487 feet above sea level. Masada's top is at sea level. On the Herodium Herod built a fortress, a palace, and a small town. He built this between 23 and 15 B.C. It is the only thing he built that bears his name.

In 40 B.C. after the Parthian conquest of Syria, Herod fled to Masada. On the way, at the location of the Herodium, Herod clashed with the Parthians and emerged victorious from this battle. According to the Roman Jewish historian Josephus, he built a town on that spot in commemoration of his victory and enhanced it with wonderful palaces ... and named it after himself.

Josephus describes it as follows:

> This fortress, which is some sixty stadia distant from Jerusalem, is naturally strong and very suitable for such a structure, for reasonably nearby is a hill raised to a greater height by the hand of man and rounded off in the shape of a breast. At intervals it has round towers, and it has a steep ascent formed of two hundred steps of hewn stone. Within it are costly royal apartments made for security and for ornament at the same time. At the base of the hill there are pleasure grounds built in such a way as to be worth seeing, among other things because of the way in which water, which is lacking in that place, is brought in from a distance and at great expense. The surrounding plain was built up as second to none, with the hill serving as an acropolis for the other dwellings.[40]

The hill crown was made higher by Herod's workmen by building four towers of stone, built on solid rock foundations and then the hill built upward enclosing a large area inside. The

---

40 *The Jewish War* I, 21, 10: *Antiquities of the Jews* XIV, chapter 13:9.

BIBLICAL ARCHAEOLOGY

raising of the hill made it possible to see from the Herodium to Masada near the Dead Sea.

When the Romans came to subjugate Israel in A.D. 71 (as spoken of by Jesus in His Olivet Discourse, Matthew 24), the Israelites led by Bar Kokhba made the Herodium their second headquarters. The Romans assaulted and destroyed much of the fort and palaces.

It was Herod's burial place, and his grave was hidden in the mountain and well disguised. One recent excavation led by Professor Ehud Netzer in May of 2007, reported they had found Herod's tomb. Since then, some others have disagreed with his findings. Netzer died from a fall at the excavation site in October of 2010.

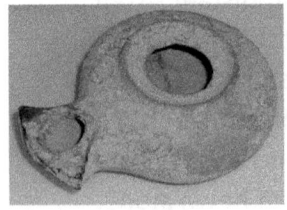

The author has in his collection of ancient artifacts, a small oil burning lamp that was found at the excavation of the Herodium. Here is a picture of this lamp.

MASADA

Masada was only recently rediscovered (1940s). From a distance it looks much like many other mountains in the Judean desert. Yet it was in this dreary and barren landscape that Herod the Great built a luxurious desert palace and fortress.

It has been called "Masada, tragic fortress in the sky." For three brave years, the freedom fighters managed to hold back 10,000 Roman troops armed with every contemporary siege weapon. Finally a battering ram breached the wall. We will come back to this later.

The author has visited this site repeatedly over a period of more than 40 years, walking the whole top of the mountain, examining the huge cisterns and water supply systems and watching the progress of the tedious work of archaeological reconstruction.

One New Year's day, which fell on Sunday, we had received permission to hold our church service in the synagogue. As we gathered to sing, read from Matthew 24 and have the Lord's Supper, Jews gathered just outside the entrance to mock us. We proceeded with calm and worshipped together the God of Israel and our Lord Jesus Christ.

The mountain is shaped like a huge ship, pointed northward. The flat-topped mesa's top is at sea level and rises 1,300 feet above the wasteland below, just west of the Dead Sea. It must be one of the most desolate spots on earth. Summer temperatures rise well above 100 degrees. From the top the view is impressive. In ancient times to ascend to the top required a difficult hike up a winding trail that was called the snake path. It winds back and forth, making its way to the top, where a massive wall and gate allowed visitors to enter.

Herod had built for himself a marvelous temple on the northern end, which was built down the side of the cliff, with a 1,000-foot drop just outside the palace walls. Inside there was a bathtub with running water, beautiful rooms with gorgeous mosaic floors, and plastered walls with bright decorations and paint. It offered the amenities of a luxurious palace in the city.

On the top above the palace was a strong wall with glacis to protect the wall to keep Herod safe. Also there were huge food, wine, and grain storage warehouses. There were saunas and swimming pools, and amenities one would never expect in this barren wilderness.

Herod's engineers had many obstacles to overcome to make this place livable. The foremost obstacle was where to get water. The area seldom gets rain, possibly one to three times a

BIBLICAL ARCHAEOLOGY

year and then in torrential downpours. There are large cisterns at the top of Masada, one big enough to play a basketball game in. This one was cut out of the solid rock. Channels were cut into the mountain top to direct this rain water into the cisterns.

To the west of the Masada Mountain are other high mountains into which the engineers made ditches that directed water down the ravines into other cisterns down inside the mountain. These channels and holes inside the mountain can still be seen. This water had to be carried from these cisterns to the top, possibly by donkeys or humans, to fill the storage reservoirs on top. Together there was enough food and water to withstand years of assault to the fortress.

With the Bar Kokhba revolt against Rome, Zealots from Jerusalem, possibly some from Qumran and other communities, gathered together on top of Masada. One thing Rome never did was give up on a battle. For three-and-one-half years the Roman garrison remained camped around Masada; they built a strong wall all the way around so the people could not escape. The Romans built a ramp all the way to the top of the mountain. This ramp was made of rocks, dirt and brush so they could assault the casemate walls and break into the fortress.

When they finally breached the wall, the 969 zealots had committed mass suicide, saying it was better to be free in death than to be a Roman slave. Only a nanny and two children survived. The zealots had burned their food storage, of which there was plenty left, and destroyed their weapons. They had cast lots to see who would kill whom and who was to be the last one to take their life. These lot tokens were found at the death site.

Outside the synagogue was a manuscript burial plot where several Old Testament manuscripts were found, along with the search associated with the finding of the Dead Sea Scrolls.

Masada is one of the very sad days in human history, but there were even worse events that took place with this Roman invasion of Israel in the A.D. 70s.

The author has a collection of biblical era coins. These begin with Alexander the Great coins about 330 B.C. and up to the twelfth century A.D. Among this collection (pictured below), is a Masada coin that was minted about A.D. 66–68, just before the destruction of Masada by the Romans. Also included are widow's mites, denarius, Emperor Constantine coins, and coins from the excavation at Petra.

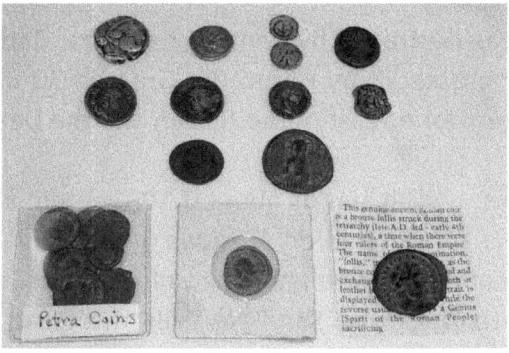

Ancient coins help show the reliability of the biblical history and help in dating archaeological excavations. Here are a few of the coins the author has collected during his nearly fifty years of travel in the Middle East.

MACHAERUS

Another of Herod's fortresses was named Machaerus. Masada and Machaerus were probably forts before Herod modernized them and built them stronger and more glorious.

Machaerus is located about 16 miles southeast of the mouth of the Jordan River where it enters the Dead Sea. This is about one third of the way down the Dead Sea on its eastern side. According to Flavius Josephus, it is the location of the imprisonment and execution of John the Baptist (see Mark 6:24 and Matthew 14:8). This infamous execution took place in A.D. 32, shortly before the Passover, following an imprisonment of two years. This was where Herod the Great's son Tetrarch Herod Antipas', second wife Princess Herodias, and her daughter, Princess Salome, were living.

Machaerus was originally built by Alexander Jannaeus who ruled from 104–78 B.C. He had built Machaerus about 90 B.C. This easily-fortified hill made it possible to watch for invaders from the east, south and north. It defended the eastern border of Israel.

The fort was destroyed by Pompey's general Gabinius in 57 B.C. and then rebuilt by Herod the Great in 30 B.C. to safeguard his territories east of the Jordan and the Dead Sea.[41]

"The hilltop, which stands about 1,100 meters above Dead Sea level, is surrounded on all sides by deep ravines which provide great natural strength. The valley on the west extends 60 stadia to the Dead Sea." He calls the Dead Sea "Lake Asphaltitis."

Herod made this a strong fort with large cisterns to collect water from the infrequent torrential downpours. It included his palace, rooms, a large courtyard and elaborate baths, and remains of the mosaic floors still can be seen. Walls, towers, and remains of a small town can be seen around the fortress.

GAMLA

The final major fortress of Herod the Great that we will examine is Gamla. Gamla is an Arabic or Hebrew word that means

---

41 Josephus gives a full description of Machaerus in his book *The Wars of the Jews* 7.6.1 ff.

camel. The fort was built on a ridge that resembled a camel's back, thus the name.

Josephus suggests that Gamla served as a part of Herod's instant warning system that covered much of Israel. The author suggested this idea to his friend Zac Jamjoum and Zac laughed at him and said, "I have lived here all my life and never heard such a thing." That day we were going to the Herodium and I said, "Well, Josephus says one can see from the Herodium to Masada and from Masada to Machaerus and on to points north to Gamla and from Gamla to the mountains of Nazareth and on to Megiddo and from Megiddo to points south in Samaria.

Zac asked what the author meant by Gamla. (Remember they were young men.) He said he had never heard of it. The author told him what Josephus had written. A couple of days later they took a $350,000 Mercedes bus up what was very much like a cow trail and they did find Gamla. This led to further research about its history.

Here is what was found. Gamla was heavily fortified and is in the Golan Heights east of the Sea of Galilee. It had been made a fort and city by a Seleucid leader during the first Syrian War in the third century B.C. It had remained populated until Josephus Flavius commanded Galilee during the Jewish revolt against Rome in A.D. 66. It was his main stronghold on the Golan Heights.

He gives a good description of this fort, saying it was on a steep hill that precluded the need to build heavy walls except along the northern saddle. This casemate wall was quite short, and was built between existing houses, which meant that the area could be more easily defended during an attack.

BIBLICAL ARCHAEOLOGY

Initially Gamla submitted to Rome but became one of only five communities that had later revolted against Rome. Rome's first attempt to take Gamla was repulsed by Josephus and his troops, but the second attempt breached the walls. Some 4,000 were slaughtered while 5,000 died by suicide, men throwing their wives and children and then jumping off the cliff. Some were trampled to death, while others jumped or were thrown to their deaths. It remains one of the darkest days of humanity along with Jerusalem's destruction and mass suicide at Masada.

Josephus was the sole survivor, found hiding by the Romans and taken captive. The rest had been killed or committed suicide. The actual number who died is open to debate, but certainly is many times more than died at Masada.

It helps to illustrate the truthfulness of the words of Jesus in Matthew 24 about a time of trouble such as the world had never seen or will see. Remember that it was in Jerusalem that the worst disaster took place. When the Romans defeated and brought into submission the Bar Kokhba revolt, most of Herod's Israel ended up in destruction.

1. In Jerusalem there was a terrible massacre.

2. At Masada there was a mass suicide of over 950 people, with only a nursemaid and two children surviving.

3. At Gamla, thousands were killed and thousands of others committed suicide.

4. Those who lived were taken to Greece to dig the Corinth Canal, to work out their lives as slaves, their existence was not much better than an animal.

5. Never has history seen its equal in brutality and people taking the lives of their own wives, children, and then killing themselves.

The Romans literally destroyed Herod's Temple, plowing the ground and digging the melted gold from the cracks in the rocks after burning the Temple and its remains.

CONCLUSIONS TO BE DRAWN

Although Masada has been said to be the most totally formidable fort ever constructed, it, along with the Herodium, Machaerus, and Gamla did not extend the life of Herod, nor stop the judgment of God on a nation that had been visited by the King of Kings and Lord of Lords, Jesus Christ the Messiah. Those who rejected Christ came to an awful end, as is eventually the case with all Christ rejecters.

The Jews who survived the destruction in A.D. 72 were taken to Greece and worked out their miserable lives digging the Corinth canal, or worked as slaves in other parts of the Roman Empire. This was a fulfillment of Jesus' prophecy in Matthew 24 about there being a terrible time of trouble such as the world had never seen.

Herod had quite a reign, had built and repaired Israel for Jesus' life and work, and then was sent to his eternal reward for his miserable and violent life of sin.

Such was the end of Sennacharib, Nebuchadnezzar and possibly even Cyrus. Of course, God will judge each person according to their deeds. We must each give an account of ourselves unto God.

BIBLICAL ARCHAEOLOGY

Yes the Bible is true, and yes, the archaeologists have documented its historical accuracy time after time. We can trust it as the Holy Bible, the inspired Word of God.

Suggested Reading:
Cornfeld, Gaalya Editor, *Josephus the Jewish War.*
Whiston, William, Translator, *Josephus Complete Works.*

Chapter Eighteen

Where We've Been and Need to Go

For seventeen chapters we have examined how archaeology has enlightened us about history and the biblical narrative. We have learned of the physical evidence to support the Bible history. This astounding information gives additional proof of the accuracy and inspiration of our Holy Bible. The biblical histories have again been verified by these archaeological explorations.

A REVIEW OF WHERE WE HAVE BEEN SO FAR

Before the flood of Noah there is little or no evidence of civilization. If we do not accept the biblical accounts, and a few other rather sketchy accounts of the early history of mankind, we are left in the dark about the ancient world before Noah. Fortunately, we do have a clear history given in our Bible.

What was the world like before Noah? How can we explain the almost total lack of archaeological evidence of civilization before the flood, and then the sudden appearance again of some of the most brilliant and literate human beings in all of history?

What happened to the rest of mankind, and how do a few humans suddenly burst on the scene? What happened to the pre-flood civilizations? Where are the graveyards? What happened to their villages and cities? Is there any explanation for these questions that makes sense? Outside the Bible there is very little coherent information.

BIBLICAL ARCHAEOLOGY

The archaeological evidence shows that civilization suddenly burst upon the scene in Mesopotamia with villages, cities, libraries, and very brilliant humans. This happened about 2450 B.C. About the same time, other ancient civilizations sprang up in China, Egypt, Europe, and the whole Middle-East, and all of this came rather suddenly.

What happened before the flood? The date of biblical creation is open to debate, but the fact of creation is not in question. The exception to this is with people who have a preconceived view they wish to propound to invalidate the biblical accounts. As Dinesh D'Souza says, "The objections to the Bible are more moral than intellectual."

For the sake of a dating beginning point, let us use Sebastian Adam's *Chronological History* chart and his dating. He suggests that creation was 1,656 years before the flood. Adams, the brilliant child prodigy and student of history, came to his time dating by studying the most ancient historians. He dates the flood of Noah at 2348 B.C. This would mean that creation was roughly 4000 B.C. These dates are open to debate, but almost certainly biblical creation would not have been later, but possibly earlier.

But with people having lived on the earth more than 1,500 years before the flood, the population would have been enormous. Remember what was said about a person being paid $1,000 for a month's work, or 1 cent doubled 30 times. Have you tried doubling a penny thirty times? Yes, the result is astounding. Such would have been the case with human population.

The most ancient Jewish histories suggest that Adam and Eve could have had as many as 60 or more children in Adam's 930 years of life. The number could have been much more. Population would have grown exponentially.

Even if children didn't reproduce until 100-plus years old, they could have continued to have children for hundreds of years, and the result would have been remarkable. John Whitcomb and Henry Morris suggest that the earth's population at the time of Noah's flood could easily have been 4–5 billion. Even if this number is high, the question remains, what happened to all these people? Where are all of these people's graveyards, cities, houses? There should be plentiful evidence for their existence. If mankind had lived on the earth for millions of years, as some suggest, where are their remains and evidence of their existence?

Again, the only plausible explanation comes from our Bibles. Could it have been a massive epidemic that wiped them out? If so, where are their graves, or bones? The lack of physical evidence for their existence points to a massive destructive event.

Remember that there is a lot of other evidence for a massive catastrophe. In the author's office is a tusk from a woolly mammoth from the permafrost of Alaska. Some massive catastrophe buried this mammoth alive.

He also has a piece of slate that came from the top of the huge coal deposits in West Virginia, USA. This slate is full of leaves and vegetation that covered the coal. Where coal is found, often there is evidence that it was put down by a massive flood, burying animal and plant matter under mud and debris that turned to slate, like hardening concrete. The coal was covered in mud filled with leaves, twigs, and remains of vegetation. Where did all this plant and animal life come from to make all this coal? What caused this massive water overflow that buried all of this?

Think of all the deposits of oil around the world. Where did all this decomposed animal and plant life come from? These oil reserves amount to trillions of millions of tons of decomposed animal and plant life. How did they get buried under hundreds or thousands of tons of rock, mud, and water-moved deposits?

This seems to suggest that at one time the earth must have been heavily covered with vegetation, huge numbers of animals, and humans, all of which were buried in a massive catastrophe. Here again the Bible history makes sense. The Hebrew word used to describe the flood was that the earth was "cataclysmed." (The author coined this word to best describe what happened.)

Here we have a plausible explanation for what happened to all of the pre-flood people and civilization. We find a reasonable explanation of why prehistoric creatures, like the dinosaurs, are found buried under water-laid clay. Being large and strong, they were able to keep above the flood waters longer than smaller and weaker animals. Being huge, they would have floated; they ended up near the top of the flood debris.

But not one graveyard, not one city, no evidence of civilization has been found prior to the flood. Supposed and very ancient human remains have again and again been proven to be frauds.

Also, do not forget that carbon 14 dating is not valid before the flood. The Bible indicates that God changed the weather and configuration of the earth after the flood. Carbon dating is based on uniformity and would not be valid after a major weather change.[42]

---

[42] If further scientific information is desired, read *Biblical Cosmology and Modern Science* and also *The Genesis Flood*, by Drs. Whitcomb and Morris.

The supposed pre-flood cities have been shown to not be from a world-wide flood but from local floods. Examples could be given of places like Ur of the Chaldees where archaeologists found houses under layers of water-laid clay. The explanation is that these houses were buried by a local flood of the Tigris and Euphrates rivers.

The Biblical account best explains why civilization explodes again in the area spreading out from Mt. Ararat. China's founder is reported to have been "Foa or Oah, who came from the great flood." This would have been who we call Noah. Yes, China's earliest civilization dates to a time not long after the Tower of Babel.

Egypt and Africa's earliest dynasties date to a time just after the Tower of Babel. India's history also dates back to a time after the confusion of languages. Ham's family moved south to Africa, Shem to Palestine and the Fertile Crescent, and Japheth moved into Europe. We have traced these civilizations for the past chapters. The biblical record has been confirmed by the archaeologists' work.

THERE IS SO MUCH WORK LEFT TO BE DONE

Here is the challenge for the next generation of Christian scientists and archaeologists. How can we explain human existence and history that is not covered in our Bible's history? Where did the Eskimos come from, or the Native Americans, the Incas, Aztecs or the people of Peru, the Hawaiian Islands, Polynesia, New Zealand, and Australia?

Even in these areas, evidence is slowly beginning to coalesce to point to their sources. Sometimes these findings are so widely separated as to not be joined together so that a logical conclusion can be drawn. Someone needs to take up this cause. Here are a few ideas that have arisen that seem to begin to join together and explain where these people came from.

DNA could be a major help in learning the origins of these distinct people groups. A group called "Living Hope Ministries," from Brigham City, Utah, produced a movie titled *DNA vs. The Book of Mormon*.

The Book of Mormon's claim is that the Native Americans were of Jewish lineage. Living Hope Ministries had DNA testing made of our Native Americans to see if they were of Jewish descent. What they learned is that Native Americans were not of Jewish descent, as claimed in the Book of Mormon, but were of Mongolian or Chinese lineage.

This would suggest that they came to America, possibly across a northern land bridge and ice flows that join North America and Europe. Some remained along the way as Eskimos. Others traveled on south. This seems to be a plausible explanation for the Eskimos and Native Americans, for there is no evidence that the American Indians were seafarers and could have come across the sea.

This raises the question as to whether the other ancient people of Central and South America could have been related. That the Native Americans and the other inhabitants of the Americas were related is the basis of exploration and writing done by Thor Heyerdahl. This led to his almost unbelievable raft trip from Peru to the Polynesian Islands.

His exploits, along with five intrepid friends, proved that ancient people could have traveled the 4,300 miles across open seas to their homes in the islands from Hawaii to Polynesia, Australia, and New Zealand. Wouldn't DNA testing be an interesting test to ascertain these people's origins?

DR. CHARLES CRANE

Heyerdahl and his friends built a balsa log raft, just like the ones in ancient folklore described by the Polynesians, using only things available to these ancient people. Then they successfully made the journey in 101 days, over 4,300 miles of open seas, with all six men surviving and arriving in good health.

Thor's book is entitled *Kon-Tiki* and recounts their adventure; it is a most exciting book and well worth reading. On page 231 in this book it tells about his original book regarding the origin of these ancient races. This book was called *American Indians in the Pacific: The History behind the Kon-Tiki Expedition*.[43]

If Heyerdahl's theory is true, then a common lineage could be shown with the Eskimos, American Indians, Aztecs, Incas, and Peruvians. It could explain where the people in North and South America came from. At this point it seems a most logical explanation.

In observing human nature, there seems to be an almost universal male trait that causes men to want to challenge new horizons, whether it is a mountain peak, sea, or some untried thrill. Often there does not seem to even need to be a reason behind this male drive. A mountain climber friend was asked why he climbed mountains. To which he replied, "Because it was there." Men seem to have an urge within that causes them to always want to explore some new vista.

So for humans to continue to press their frontiers outward and explore what is across the next hill or mountain is quite understandable. This trait of human nature would explain the constant pressure to move across the earth. God had com-

---

[43] *Kon-Tiki*, Pocket Books, a division of Simon & Schuster, Inc., 630 Fifth Avenue, New York, NY. 1950.

manded people to be fruitful and fill the earth. Would He have commanded them to do what was impossible?

Additional information seems to indicate that there are similarities between the Mesopotamia temple buildings and those found in Central and South America. Could there be a historical connection somewhere in the past? There is a striking similarity between the ziggurats of Mesopotamia, pyramids of Egypt, and the Central American temples. Could there be a connection? This question is interesting and needs further exploration.

So, people could have traveled from China to Mongolia, across Russia, the Bering Straits, to Alaska, south to North America, Central America, and on to South America.

The question that bothered Thor Heyerdahl was how to explain the origin of people in the Hawaiian Islands, Samoa, Polynesia, and onward. Thor, as a young man, had visited Polynesia and been charmed by the ancient legends of how they had gotten to the islands so far away from the rest of civilization. This led to his research. He developed a hypothesis that they must have come over the seas from somewhere else.

The most ancient tradition of these people was that they had come by rafts from a country with high mountains that were to the east. His research led him to believe this place of origin was Peru or somewhere in South America.

Several facts led him to this conclusion. One of which was that prevailing currents and winds would make it possible to sail a raft from Peru to these islands. It would have had to be a raft since they had no ocean-going boats. He conjectured that they had sailed their rafts across the 4,300 miles of open sea to the many Islands.

DR. CHARLES CRANE

When Thor Heyerdahl tried to sell the manuscript that he had written about these people being related to the American Indians, he was met by total unbelief. In trying get his book published, one publisher challenged him to prove his theory by doing it. He accepted this challenge, and the result is an account of one of the most astounding and almost unbelievable sea adventures ever accomplished. In his book Kon-Tiki he tells the story of this sea adventure.

In short, he and five buddies, none of which were sailors, studied the ancient Peruvian histories and learned about the rafts made of balsa wood logs that these people used to fish the rather treacherous waters off their western coast.

Again, they were men and there was a frontier to explore. And so these ancient seamen, with the male trait of "if it is there let's try it," set out to explore. Whether it was on purpose or by accident is not known, but Thor believed they had made the journey 4,300 miles across the open ocean to their new homes on purpose. For them to have survived the trip they would have had to have done careful planning. He and five friends set out to prove his theory using only the things the ancient people had.

The whole process was fraught with almost impossible challenges. One by one these obstacles were overcome and finally they set off on what turned into a 101-day cruise across open water in their balsa wood raft.

The trip was not only possible, but achieved by amateur seamen. They had used nothing that was not available to prehistoric Peruvians. Each of them arrived safe and sound.

Yes, the inhabitants of the islands of the sea could have, and probably did, come from those intrepid pioneers whose roots reach clear back to their most ancient ancestor Foa, Oah, or Noah, who founded China more than 2,000 years before Christ. These Polynesian pioneers did their work somewhere around A.D. 500. The actual date of these adventurers is yet to be firmly determined.

Heyerdahl and his buddies found many words, events, plants and names that were the same as in Peru and the Polynesian islands. It seems impossible that he had not found the origin of those who dwell on the islands of the seas. He found food plants with identical names, trees with the same names, carvings, and statues that were very similar in both places. He found the same trees, plants, and vegetables in both places. The list of similarities could be much longer.

A lot of work needs to be done to connect many additional dots so as to be able to draw an actual history of these ancient people and their migrations over the earth.

CONCLUSIONS

The Bible has had many tests applied to it—the test of fulfilled prophecy, the test of science, the test of accuracy, the test of textual purity, the test of history—the list could go on and on. This study and examination has been the test of archaeology. Repeatedly the places and people told about in our Bible have been found by the archaeologists. Our Bible has not only survived the test of archaeology, but has been proven to be supernaturally accurate.

The comparison between the Bible history and other ancient histories shows a vast difference. Non-biblical histories are filled with errors, nonsense, and scientific inaccuracies. The incredible accuracy of the Bible can best be explained by its divine inspiration. The Apostle Paul said in II Timothy 3:16–17: "All scripture is given by inspiration of God ..." Jesus said in John 10:35: "... the scriptures cannot be broken." The Bible stands!

DR. CHARLES CRANE

THE BIBLE STANDS

The Bible stands like a rock undaunted
'Mid the raging storms of time;
Its pages burn with the truth eternal,
And they glow with a light sublime.

The Bible stands though the hills may tumble,
It will firmly stand when the earth shall crumble;
I will plant my feet on its firm foundation,
For the Bible stands.

The Bible stands like a mountain tow'ring
Far above the works of men;
Its truth by none ever was refuted,
And destroy it they never can.

The Bible stands and it will forever,
When the world has passed away;
By inspiration it has been given,
All its precepts I will obey.

The Bible stands every test we give it,
For its Author is divine;
By grace alone I expect to live it,
And to prove and to make it mine.

The Bible stands though the hills may tumble,
It will firmly stand when the earth shall crumble;
I will plant my feet on its firm foundation,
For the Bible stands.
Haldor Lillenas

BIBLICAL ARCHAEOLOGY

Suggested Reading:

Heyerdahl, Thor, *Kon-Tiki*.
Watch the video, *DNA vs. The Book of Mormon*.

BIBLIOGRAPHY

Adams, Sebastian C., *Synchronological Chart of World History*.

The Bible, English Standard Version, Crossway, Wheaton, Illinois, Copyright 2001.

Biblical Archaeology Review, The Archives, 1975–2012.

Blum, Howard, *The Gold of Exodus, The Discovery of the True Mount Sinai*, Simon & Schuster, Rockefeller Center, 1230 Ave of the Americas, New York, NY 10020, 1998.

Basliger, Dave and Sellier, Charles E. Jr., *In Search of Noah's Ark*, Sun Classic books, 11071 Massachusetts Ave., Los Angeles, CA 90025, 1976.

Browning, Iain, *Petra*, 1982, Chatto and Windus, Ltd., 40 William IV Street, London WC2N 4DF.

Ceram, C.W. *Gods, Graves and Scholars*, Bantam Books, Copyright 1967, Alfred A. Knopf, Inc., New York, NY, 10022.

Cornfeld, Gaalyah, and Freedman, David Noel, *Archaeology of the Bible Book by Book*. Harper and Row, Publishers, San Francisco, Cambridge, Hagerstown, New York, Philadelphia, London, Mexico City, Sao Paulo, Sidney, Copyright 1976.

BIBLICAL ARCHAEOLOGY

Crane, Charles A., *The Bible: The True and Reliable Word of God*, Second Printing 2014, Copyright Charles A. Crane, Endurance Press, 577 N. Cardigan, Ave, Star, Idaho.

Crane, Charles A., Over forty years of visitation of archaeological sites discussed, Israel, Jordan, Syria, Lebanon, Egypt, Sinai, Turkey, and Greece.

The Dead Sea Scrolls, Time Inc. Books, 225 Liberty Street, New York, NY 10281, 2016.

DNA and the Book of Mormon, Living Hope Ministries, Brigham City, Utah, 2003.

Everyday Life in Bible Times, National Geographic Society, Copyright 1967, referenced but not quoted.

Giovanni, Pettinato, *The Archives of Ebla, An Empire Inscribed in Clay*, Doubleday and Company Inc., 1981.

Gonzalo, Baez-Camargo, *From Genesis to Revelation ... Archaeological Commentary on the Bible*. American Bible Society, Doubleday and Company, Inc., Garden City, New York, 1984.

Halley, Henry H., *Bible Handbook*, Henry H. Halley, Box 774, Chicago 90, Illinois, 1951.

Heyerdahl, Thor, *Kon-Tiki*, Washington Square Press Enriched Classics, Pocket Books, Rand McNalley editor, New York, 1950.

Josephus Complete Works, Kregel Publications, Grand Rapids, Michigan 49501, 1980.

DR. CHARLES CRANE

Josephus, *The Jewish War*, Gaalya Cornfeld, Zondervan Publishing House, Grand Rapids, Michigan 49506, 1982.

Kenyon, Kathleen M., *The Bible and Recent Archaeology*, British Museum Publishers, Ltd, 46 Bloomsbury Street, London WC1B 3QQ, 1978.

Martin, Dr. James C., *Preserving Bible Times*.

Matthiae, Paolo, *Ebla, An Empire Rediscovered*, Doubleday & Company, Inc., Garden City, New York, 1980.

McDowell, Josh, *Evidence That Demands a Verdict*, Campus Crusade, San Bernadena CA, 1972.

Morris and Whitcomb, *The Genesis Flood*, The Presbyterian and Reformed Publishing Company, Philadelphia, Pennsylvania, 1975.

Morris, Henry M., *Biblical Cosmology and Modern Science*, Craig Press, Nutley, New Jersey, 1967.

NIV Archaeological Study Bible, Copyright 1984, Zondervan.

Wikipedia and other on line sources, especially for photos.

Other Books by Dr. Charles Crane

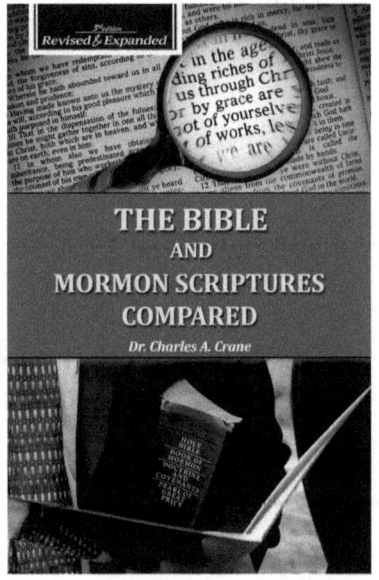

For ordering info visit:

www.endurancepress.com

www.ingramcontent.com/pod-product-compliance
Lightning Source LLC
Chambersburg PA
CBHW071705090426
42738CB00009B/1669